WINGS

of

WISDOM

*Your Daily Guide to
Benefit from Change,
Profit from Failure,
and Design Your
Own Destiny!*

Catherine Pulsifer

This book is designed to provide information and guidance in regard to the subject matter covered. It is sold with the understanding that the publisher and author are not engaged in rendering counseling, legal, or other professional services.

The quotations shown in the book have been collected for many years from various sources. Attempts to ensure their accuracy have been made. If, however, you find any that are incorrect, please advise the publisher, and they will be corrected in the next reprint.

Anncath-Roby Books
P.O. Box 21085
Mississauga ON Canada L5N 6A2

Canadian Cataloguing in Publication Data

Pulsifer, Catherine, 1957 -
Wings of wisdom :
your daily guide to benefit from change, profit from
failure, and design your own destiny!

Includes bibliographical references and index.

ISBN 0-9683013-0-4

1. Self-actualization (Psychology) - Quotations, maxims, etc. I. Title

BF637.S4P84 1998   158.1   C98-930743-3

Cover Design by G. Robertson

Printed and bound in Canada

Contents

Contents

Introduction

Fifteen years ago, I hit a brick wall. I had a job I hated that was literally making me sick. My marriage was in trouble; my finances were a disaster; and, I lived many miles away from my family.

I felt I had hit bottom. The easy way out would have been to feel sorry for myself and blame the world for my misfortune, to moan and groan about how unfair life is.

Instead, I found my way to the public library and discovered a new world in the self-help section. It focused my energy on positive results, rather than on the "poor me" syndrome. I started reading books on setting goals, positive thinking, psychology, auto-biographies, attitudes, and so on.

At that time, I started to collect quotes. I discovered that certain quotes made me stop and think; they made me challenge my beliefs, while others gave me hope.

Without realizing it, I was searching for answers. Why are some people more successful than others?

How do they cope with challenges? Other people had more serious problems than I did. How did they keep a positive attitude and overcome their problems?

Through all my years of reading and research, I found two consistent qualities of successful people:

Attitude, and Goals.

Attitude

A "positive attitude" is definitely one of the keys to success.

My definition of a positive attitude is a simple one:

Looking for the good in all circumstances.

Applying it to everyday life is not as simple as it seems. Some situations in life challenge us to see the good. For example, the death of someone close to us, a health problem, the loss of a job, a relationship that doesn't work out. It is difficult to maintain a positive attitude in these situations.

If you accept what has happened and search for the positive, you will be able to move forward in your life. By embracing this attitude, you eliminate the "poor me syndrome". Attitudes play a very important role in our lives.

How do you react when faced with:
- change
- challenges
- failures
- stress

• Change
In today's society, change is constant. Although change has always occurred in every society, today it is much more rapid due to technological advancements and a global market.

If you resist change, you will face challenges on a daily basis. If you consciously refocus your attitude to see the benefits of change, your outlook becomes positive and life becomes easier.

• Challenges
We all face challenges. How we react to them is what really makes a big difference. Some people overreact and make mountains out of the proverbial mole hill. Facing our challenges head on and setting goals to take us through and beyond the challenge, helps us cope with the hurtles we all confront.

There is nothing worse than being unable to see light at the end of the tunnel. I have learned to focus my energies on solutions, not on the challenge itself. So often, I have seen people waste energy by moaning and groaning about a problem. Yet, if they just realigned their attitude and focused on the solution or on the opportunity, the challenge would not seem as big as they think it is.

- **Failure**

How do you see failure?

If you accept failure as an opportunity to learn, it will change your whole perspective. Some people allow failures to stop them from ever attempting anything new. Rather than learn and move on, these people get stuck forever.

- **Stress**

Today, we hear over and over again that people are stressed. Stress, however, is created by our attitude. How we perceive a situation and how we react to it is the basis of our stress. If you focus on the negative in any situation, you can expect high stress levels. However, if you try and see the good in the situation, your stress levels will greatly diminish.

I attended a course on stress where the instructor explained that we create our own "stressors". We actually create our own stress by our perception of events. Yes, there are external events that cause us concern, but how we perceive the event determines the stress we feel. That thought has stayed with me over the years. When I feel overwhelmed and my stress levels rise, I stop and step back from the situation and put the event in perspective. I always ask myself — what difference will this make in five years time? Most of the time, it will not make any significant difference in my life. Just answering that question helps reduce my stress level. For those events that will make a difference in five years, I reduce stress by focusing my energy on *finding solutions*.

<u>Goals</u>

As you read this book, you will see how strong my belief is in setting goals. I set a goal 10 years ago for my professional career and surpassed it a few years ago. One of my more recent goals was to write this book. My goals kept me focused. As a result, you are now reading what was once only a thought, a dream!

Goals do work!

The easiest way to set goals is to answer the following questions:
- What is it I want to achieve?
- When do I want to achieve it?
- Where am I today and what action do I need to take to achieve my goal?

Write down your answers. Writing out your goals is as important as determining what they are. You are committing yourself to achieve these goals and, at the same time, sending a strong, positive message to your subconscious mind.

- **What is it I want to achieve?**

There are various ways to determine this. One way to answer this question is to write down the things you consistently wish for. Be specific. For example, the type of job you want; how much money you want to earn; the type of relationships you want to have; where you want to live; the kind of house you want to live in; what type of car you want to drive, and so on.

Another method is to write goals by category: career, financial, family, leisure, educational, vacation, spiritual, and so on.

There are many excellent books on goal setting in the "recommended reading" list at the back

of this book. Your local library will have some
of these books.

- **When do I want to achieve it?**
There are two types of goals:
- short term goals (1-2 years)
- long term goals (5-10 years)

Your short term goals should support your
long term goals. Let me point out, however,
that over time, your long term goals may
change. If so, adjust your short term goals to
support your long term. Goals should be
flexible, not carved in stone!

Having said that, the time period you give
yourself to finish your goal is still important.
Time frames help you stay focused by giving
you milestones by which to measure your
progress. By committing to a time frame, you
are making a commitment to yourself. We can
easily be side-tracked after we set goals. A
written commitment will help keep you on
track.

- **Where am I today and what action do I
  need to take to achieve my goal?**
The most important step in goal setting is
taking action. You can decide on your goal
and you can write it down, but unless you take
action the goal is useless.

In order to achieve a goal, you need to identify the actions you must take. For example, in what areas will additional knowledge be required? What areas will you have to develop or learn new skills?

As you work on your goals, you should also review your progress. I usually review my goals every six months. I determine if I am on track, if I need to make adjustments, and if my goals and time frames are realistic. By doing this, you are actually charting your own progress. It always gives me a sense of self-achievement, and allows me to renew my commitment to my future goals. If I am not on target, I make the necessary adjustments. The most important thing is that I am moving forward even if I am not always progressing at the speed I originally planned.

Goals allow you to see light at the end of the tunnel, whether that light be a new career, a promotion, a prosperous business, or advanced training. You may not be where you want to be today, but by setting goals you are changing your life and moving toward where you want to be.

When people find themselves in situations with

little or no hope, they give up. They convince themselves they are satisfied with where they are, or what they have.

Goals give us hope!

For me, goals are my road map to the life I want. They have helped me accomplish things I once thought were impossible.

What is interesting about goals is that once you are committed and start to implement your plan, you will make important discoveries just by keeping a focus on attaining your desired result.

In the next 30 days, examine your own attitudes and review or set your goals. Also read the daily quotations and thoughts and reflect on how they could help to change your life. At the end of 30 days, my hope is that this book will start to make a positive difference in your life.

Many of the quotes in this book have inspired, motivated, and helped me positively change my life. They have given me a much needed different perspective on many situations that I have encountered over the years.

It is my hope that this book will help you to make positive and rewarding changes in your life!
Catherine Pulsifer

This book is dedicated to
Curtis and Julie Butler

*May the thoughts in this book help
you both as you travel through the
journey of life!*

*The two of you are my
inspiration and my joy!*

Acknowledgements

*I would like to express my thanks, appreciation, and gratitude to **Nancy Allinotte**, **Vern Coxhead**, **Bryan Glendinning**, **Jill Hepburn**, **Michael Lowe**, **Brenda McCann**, **Sandra Martin**, **Rizwana Shaikh**, **Bertha Spicer**, **Ron Stupen**, and **Michael Wilson**. I realize all of you took time from your already busy lives to read my book and give me your feedback. Your comments inspired me and helped me to continue! From the bottom of my heart,*
THANK YOU!

*And a special thank you to **Margie Lockhart** whose professional editorial comments were of great assistance!*

*Sometimes, we all need someone to support us, to believe in us, and to encourage us. I was very fortunate to have a person who gave me that. Thank you, **Byron!** Also, thank you for the numerous times you helped edit the book!*

*"Books are but waste paper
unless we spend in action the
wisdom we get from them."*
Edward G. Bulwer-Lytton

January

JANUARY 1

*"From your parents you learn love
and laughter and how to put one
foot before the other.
But when books are opened you
discover you have wings."*
Helen Hayes

The wings of life are like those of a butterfly.

As a child, we are protected and guided by our parents like a cocoon protecting a butterfly. Later, we test our own wings, sometimes fluttering, falling or soaring to great heights.

Our ability to achieve success depends on the strength of our wings gained through knowledge and experience. The greater our knowledge and experience, the higher we can fly.

***May the writings in this book
challenge and reinforce your wings!***

1

January 2

"That some achieve great success,
is proof to all that others can
achieve it as well."
Abraham Lincoln

January 3

"Fear less, hope more;
eat less, chew more;
whine less, breathe more;
talk less, say more;
hate less, love more;
and all good things are yours."
Swedish Proverb

*"How old would you be if you
didn't know how old you was."*
Satchel Paige

If we did not know our age, some of us
would appear to be very young, and
some of us would seem very old.

Sometimes, people use age as a convenient
excuse. "I'm too old to start something
new", or, "I couldn't learn that at my age."
Other people, though, go on to achieve
their greatest accomplishments in life in
later years. Take, for example, Colonel
Harland Sanders who started franchising
his chicken outlets when he was 65 years
old. Up to the age of 90 years old he
traveled 250,000 miles a year visiting KFC
franchises. He not only overcame personal
and business adversities, but more
importantly, he didn't let age stand in his
way!

Feelings lead to attitudes, attitudes become
beliefs, and beliefs become the basis for
actions. It is not important how old you are;
it is how you feel, how you think, and what
you do that is important.

JANUARY 5

*"Nobody grows old by merely
living a number of years. People
grow old by deserting their ideals.
Years may wrinkle the skin, but to
give up wrinkles the soul."*
General Douglas MacArthur

JANUARY 6

*"Age is an issue of mind over
matter.
If you don't mind, it doesn't
matter."*
Mark Twain

January 7

*"The fool wonders,
the wise man asks."*
Benjamin Disraeli

Some people won't ask a simple question because they're afraid they will appear foolish. Asking questions though, is one of the fundamental keys to learning. It is always better to ask a question than pretend you understand.

You may have heard a teacher say, "There is no such thing as a stupid question". By not asking questions, you are limiting your decision making ability. Without a full understanding of the issues, you may make an inappropriate decision.

By asking a question, you gain both information and clarity which, in turn, allows you to grow.

You may have found that the question you asked in meetings has also been an unspoken question from others. So, by asking questions, you not only help yourself, but you are also helping others to increase their understanding.

January 8

"If you don't know, ask.
You will be a fool for the moment,
but a wise man for the rest of your
life."
Seneca

January 9

"How do you know so much about
everything? was asked of a very
wise and intelligent man; and the
answer was
'By never being afraid or ashamed
to ask questions as to anything of
which I was ignorant'."
John Abbott

January 10

"The world hates change,
yet it is the only thing that
has brought progress."
Charles F. Kettering

I have worked with many people who hate any kind of change. They prefer to leave everything as it is because they feel secure and comfortable with the way things are.

We need change, yet, we often resist it for any number of reasons.

Imagine how stagnant the world would be without change — we would not have cars, dishwashers, planes, or computers. Change brings progress.

Change *is* going to happen whether we like it or not. Look forward to it as a friend not as a foe, see change as opportunity.

In our world today, we must be able to adapt. One way to cope is to focus on the benefits of the change, rather than on the negative aspects.

January 11

*"Change is as inexorable as time,
yet nothing meets with more
resistance."*

Benjamin Disraeli

January 12

*"There is nothing
permanent except change."*

Heraclitus

"I've seen many troubles in my time, only half of which ever came true."

Mark Twain

Worrying about issues unnecessarily can cause both psychological and physical distress. A lot of times, what we worry about never comes true.

When you find yourself worrying, ask yourself, "Can I do anything about it?" If you can, then take the required action to eliminate the worry. If you can't do anything about it, or if it is beyond your control, then don't waste your time worrying!

When you worry, you are not focused on solutions. You are allowing unproductive negative thinking to overrule your positive thinking. Worrying never leads to any productive results, it only reinforces the negative.

The only thing you will ever accomplish by worrying is to elevate your stress level.

January 14

*"When I look back on all the
worries I remember the story of the
old man who said on his deathbed
that he had a lot of trouble in his
life, most of which never
happened."*

Winston Churchill

January 15

*"Worry a little bit every day and in
a lifetime you will lose a couple of
years.
If something is wrong, fix it if you
can. But train yourself not to
worry:
Worry never fixes anything."*

Ernest Hemingway

"If one does not know to which port one is sailing, no wind is favourable."

Seneca

G oals allow you to set a clear direction to move forward to your chosen port.

Goals allow you to focus your energy to your advantage. They are your personal statements of what you want to achieve and how you choose to spend your time. But, without goals, you can drift aimlessly, going from one thing to another, never achieving success.

Goals enable you to:
- achieve more because you are focused
- improve your self-confidence by seeing what you have accomplished
- have a sense of self-satisfaction.

One secret to remember is to set realistic goals. Don't set so many goals that you will feel overwhelmed.

Design your life, set your goals!

JANUARY 17

*"A man without a purpose is like
a ship without a rudder."*

Thomas Carlyle

JANUARY 18

*"I find the great thing in this world
is not so much where we stand,
as in what direction we are
moving...
we must sail sometimes with the
wind and
sometimes against it ...
but we must sail and
not drift nor lie at anchor."*

Oliver Wendell Holmes

JANUARY 19

*"The mind grows by
what it feeds on."*

J. G. Holland

On what do you feed your mind?

One of my major concerns today is that a lot of people feed their mind with television. We increasingly judge our success and personal worth by television stories — stories of the rich and famous, those who have beauty and the perfect body, those who do little work and still succeed. Yet, this is not reality.

You can lose your job, you can lose material items, but you can never lose your knowledge. The money we invest in ourselves to further increase our knowledge is truly an investment in our future.

How many self improvement books have you read over the last year? How many educational programs have you listened to that have helped you learn something new?

***What have you fed
your mind in the last month?***

JANUARY 20

"If a man empties his purse into his head, no man can take it away from him.
An investment in knowledge always pays the best interest."
Benjamin Franklin

JANUARY 21

"As a field, however fertile, cannot be fruitful without cultivation, neither can a mind without learning."
Marcus Tullius Cicero

JANUARY 22

"Life's most urgent question is:
what are you doing for others?"
Martin Luther King Jr.

No one can go through life alone. We all need help or assistance at some point in our lives.

Sometimes, our lives seem so busy that we do not take time to stop and lend a helping hand. We should always be willing to offer assistance, for we never know when we will need assistance.

If someone asked you, "what have you done today for someone else", what would your response be?

One of the greatest satisfactions in life is to help someone else, to teach, to share your knowledge, or to provide a receptive sounding board.

I sincerely believe that all we do for others comes back to us in many positive ways.

January 23

"Do something for somebody every
day for which you do not get paid."
Albert Schweitzer

January 24

"I expect to pass through life but
once.
If, therefore, there be any
kindness I can show,
or if any good thing I can do to any
fellow being,
let me do it now, and not defer or
neglect it,
as I shall not pass this way
again."
William Penn

*Speak with confidence
and believe in yourself!*

After many years of working, I have encountered some exceptionally bright people. Regardless of their intelligence, however, some of them do not believe in themselves. I can easily tell that by the way they talk because they use phrases such as:

- this may be a stupid question...
- this probably won't work...
- I have a solution, but it may not help...

What they are actually doing is setting themselves up for a negative reaction. In fact, they are helping others find a reason to reject their idea. Usually, their idea is a great one!

Listen to the words you speak. If you catch yourself using negative words or phrases, change them to positive ones!

**Believe in yourself and
have confidence in your ideas.**

January 26

*"Keep away from people who try to
belittle your ambitions. Small
people always do that, but the
really great make you feel that
you, too, can become great."*

Mark Twain

January 27

*"Make the most of yourself,
for that is all there is of you."*

Ralph Waldo Emerson

*"I am only one, but still I am one.
I cannot do everything, but still I
can do something; and because I
cannot do everything, I will not
refuse to do something I can do."*
Edward Everett Hale

You do make a difference.

A story I heard many years ago, tells of
how one person made a difference.

Early one evening a man was walking
along a beach when he saw a boy picking
up starfish and flinging them into the sea.
The man asked the boy why he was doing
this. The boy explained the starfish would
die if left to the morning. The man asked
the boy, "What difference will your efforts
make when there are thousands of starfish
on the beach?" The boy stopped and
looked at the starfish he was holding and
said, "It will make a difference to this one."

There are a countless number of
opportunities where you can make a
difference every day!

January 29

"Don't wait for extraordinary
circumstance to do good;
try to use ordinary situations."
Charles Richter

January 30

"Do what you can,
with what you have,
where you are."
Theodore Roosevelt

"When you come to the end of your
rope, tie a knot and hang on."
Franklin D. Roosevelt

Don't let go of your dreams. If you have determination and belief in your dreams, you will succeed in spite of your desire to let go.

One notable person who demonstrated this attitude was Washington Roebling. He and his father had a dream of building a suspension bridge. Not long after starting construction, his father died. Washington carried on but was struck with the paralyzing caisson disease. It was impossible for him to go to the site. But, possessed with a dream, a strong desire, and with the help of his wife, Emily, he was able to complete the Brooklyn Bridge.

Here was a man who suffered the death of his father and became paralyzed, yet, he did not give up on his dreams!

"People seldom see the halting and painful steps by which the most insignificant success is achieved."

Anne Sullivan

February

"The dictionary is the only place where success comes before work."

Mark Twain

Would you expect to get heat from a wood stove without putting wood in it? Would you expect your car to run without putting gas in it? Would you expect to withdraw money from your bank account without ever having made a deposit?

While the answers to these questions are very obvious, there are people who expect success without ever putting in any work or effort!

One of the common traits of successful people is their understanding of the importance of time, effort, and commitment to achieve success!

Make sure your dictionary on life shows work before success!

FEBRUARY 2

*"There is no substitute
for hard work."*
Thomas A. Edison

FEBRUARY 3

*"If people knew how hard I worked
to achieve my mastery, it wouldn't
seem so wonderful after all."*
Michelangelo

FEBRUARY 4

*"Treat a man as he is and he will
remain as he is.
Treat a man as he can and should
be and he will become as he can
and should be."*

Geothe

People have a tendency to live up to our expectations.

If you expect little of a person, that is what you will get. How you treat people is very often how they will act in return, the old "self fulfilling prophecy".

When we see people as important, we interact with them in a pleasant tone of voice and positive attitude. How often have we been guilty of seeing people as they are today, and treating them as if they will always be that way.

Why not look for the positive qualities and the potential in everyone. It will not only change your outlook and behaviour towards them, but, more importantly, it will give people encouragement to develop to their fullest potential.

FEBRUARY 5

"I always prefer to believe
the best of everybody —
it saves so much trouble."
Rudyard Kipling

FEBRUARY 6

"There is something that is much
more scarce,
something finer far, something
rather than ability.
It is the ability to recognize ability."
Elbert Hubbard

*Plans are not just for
constructing buildings,
plans are for building your life.
What do you plan for?*

Do you spend more time planning a
vacation than you do planning your
life? In reality, most people spend a lot
more time planning their vacations. They
compile different vacation options, the
prices, when they will go, how long they
will stay, and what they will do.

Imagine what would happen if you
planned your career with as much thought
and detail. Just think what you could
accomplish if you wrote down your career
aspirations, how much money you wanted
to make, what you needed to study, what
courses you would have to take, and the
time frames for each. In other words, you
plan by setting precise goals.

If you were to set goals for each area of
your life, just think how focused you
would be. Your achievements would
astound you!

FEBRUARY 8

*What would you do if you were
guaranteed that you would
achieve success?
What would you choose for a
career if money didn't matter?*

FEBRUARY 9

*"There is only one success —
to be able to spend your life
in your own way."*
Christopher Morley

FEBRUARY **10**

In keeping an open mind,
you will learn new things by
openly challenging your beliefs
and attitudes.

Keeping an open mind by truly
listening allows us to see a new, or
different picture.

Most of us are guilty of having
preconceived ideas. We may believe a new
way won't work, or we may assume it has
already been tried before. We close our
minds before we even hear the whole
story.

To have an open mind takes courage. It
means allowing our ideas, thoughts, and
beliefs to be challenged. It also takes active
listening skills, and the ability to see things
as they could be rather than as they are, or
as they used to be!

Sometimes, we accept things the way they
are, rather than looking at the way it could
be.

FEBRUARY 11

*An open mind will allow
your ears to see things
that your eyes cannot.*

FEBRUARY 12

*"Discovery consists of seeing what
everybody has seen and thinking
what nobody has thought."*
Dr. Albert Szent-Gyorgyi

"Nobody makes a greater mistake
than he who does nothing because
he could only do a little."
Edmund Burke

If everyone would only do just a little,
imagine what a difference it would make
in the world.

Take recycling, for example. It is successful
because a lot of people are each doing a
little. If we all took the position that what
we could do would be too little, we
wouldn't be experiencing the progress we
are today.

Similarly, when you first begin a project,
you may only have enough time to do a
little. Over time, however, what may first
appear to be small efforts will multiply
and end up being significant!

If inventors and scientists just gave up
because they didn't have enough time, or
didn't have all the answers, imagine all the
conveniences, or advances in medicine, we
would not have today!

Personal action is your pathway to
success!

FEBRUARY 14

"If it fails, admit it frankly and try another. But above all, try something."

Franklin D. Roosevelt

FEBRUARY 15

"If there is no wind, row."

Latin Proverb

FEBRUARY 16

*"If you have made mistakes...
there is always another
chance for you...
you may have a fresh start
any moment you choose,
for this thing we call 'Failure'
is not the falling down,
but the staying down."*
Mary Pickford

A much better perspective on failure — a chance for a fresh start! The most important point here is *"choice"* because you decide how you view your failure, you decide if you stay down.

There are many stories of people who chose not to stay down:
- The Beatles' first audition — the recording company rejected them.
- Lucille Ball, the actress, was told to try another profession.
- Authors who have received numerous rejection slips, but they kept going until they were published.

***Remember, how you view
"failure" is entirely up to you.***

FEBRUARY 17

"Failure is the opportunity to begin again more intelligently."
Henry Ford

FEBRUARY 18

"In any moment of decision the best thing you can do is the right thing, the next best thing is the wrong thing, and the worst thing you can do is nothing."
Theodore Roosevelt

*"One that would have the
fruit must climb the tree."*
Thomas Fuller

In order to *"climb the tree"*, to achieve
success, we must be willing to expand
our knowledge, and change our mindset.
The information era we live in today has
changed drastically from the industrial
age.

Not that long ago, the expectation was you
would show up for work every day, stay
with one company for 25 years, and then
retire. Today, you must be willing to take
responsibility for your actions. No longer
is top management the only group held
accountable. You must take responsibility
to develop new skills. You must be flexible
and embrace change.

***There is still fruit on the tree, but you
must prepare yourself for the climb.
Do not count on yesterday's methods to
lead you to success today!***

FEBRUARY 20

*"No bird soars too high if he
soars with his own wings."*
William Blake

FEBRUARY 21

*"Hold yourself responsible
for a higher standard than
anyone expects of you.
Never excuse yourself."*
Henry Ward Beecher

FEBRUARY 22

*"The man who does not
read books has no
advantage over the man
that cannot read."*
Mark Twain

Those who are illiterate miss so much in
life, and yet, an even sadder situation
is the literate who never reads. So much
can be learned and enjoyed from reading.
Reading allows your mind to grow and
ignites your imagination.

To a great extent, TV has replaced reading,
especially for adolescents. The problem is
that TV diminishes the active use of your
mind. Your mind becomes lazy because
everything is presented to you.

Successful people are self- educated
whether it be new technology or new
developments in their field.

Ask someone you consider successful what
books they have read over the last year.

FEBRUARY 23

*"All men who have turned
out worth anything have
had the chief hand in their
own education."*
Sir Walter Scott

FEBRUARY 24

*"I would rather live in a
world where my life is
surrounded by mystery
than live in a world so
small that my mind
could comprehend it."*
Harry Fosdick

Your attitude can take you forward
or
your attitude can take you down.
The choice is always yours!

A ttitude determines **everything**!

How we react, what we do or say, all depends on our attitude. It determines whether we'll be happy or sad. Attitude can help, or hinder us in all areas of our lives.

If your thoughts are constantly of doom and gloom, you will receive the same in return.

Your thoughts and your perception of the world influences all that you do, and all that you are, and all that you can be.

Changing your attitude is really changing the way you see things. To begin the change, you must start looking for the good in every situation, rather than the negative.

FEBRUARY 26

"You cannot be healthy;
you cannot be happy;
you cannot be prosperous;
if you have a bad disposition."
Emmet Fox

FEBRUARY 27

"The greatest discovery of
my generation is that
a human being can alter
his life by altering
his attitude."
William James

*"A journey of a thousand miles
begins with a single step."*
Chinese Proverb

When I first thought about compiling and writing this book, the task seemed overwhelming — what quotes to use, what thoughts to share, the typing involved, the indexing, the editing and reediting. Where would I find the time required?

It was the first step, reviewing the quotes I had collected, that started me on this journey.

If the only thing I did was to think about this book, it would never have been published. By taking that first step, reviewing my written goals and moving forward one step at a time, I was able to successfully complete this book.

Whatever your journey, take that first step, then, one step at a time, and you will be amazed at what *you can accomplish!*

*"Enthusiasm...
the sustaining power of
all great action."*
Samuel Smiles

March

MARCH 1

*"A man can succeed at almost
anything for which he has
unlimited enthusiasm."*
Charles M. Schwab

If you approach any task without
enthusiasm, the task will be laborious.
With enthusiasm, any task becomes so
much easier.

Enthusiasm can be contagious. When you
work with enthusiastic people, you can't
help but be enthusiastic yourself.
Enthusiasm spreads like wild fire.

Think of people you have worked with.
Usually, those who show enthusiasm are
fun to work with. And, those who have
little enthusiasm usually bring you down.

I have a post-card on my desk taken from
"Life's Little Instruction Book" that says:
"Be the most enthusiastic and positive
person you know!" When I am having a
difficult day, I read that card, and it
encourages me to change my outlook.

March 2

*"Nothing great was ever achieved
without enthusiasm."*
Ralph Waldo Emerson

March 3

*"If you are not fired with
enthusiasm,
you will be fired with enthusiasm."*
Vince Lombardi

MARCH 4

"Live your beliefs and you can turn the world around."
Henry David Thoreau

Think of all the people who changed the world because they *"lived their beliefs"* - Thomas Edison; Alexander Bell; Martin Luther King Jr; Helen Keller; Mother Theresa — the list goes on and on! These people changed our world.

Belief gives us a foundation from which to build great accomplishments. Our beliefs help us overcome obstacles by allowing our minds to discover new avenues. New ideas, new strategies are constantly unveiled as we move towards our goal. Ideas put in motion change our world.

In order for you to accomplish anything, the foremost belief you must possess is a **belief in yourself.**

Once you believe in yourself, you can then **"turn your world around"!**

March 5

*"Nothing will ever be attempted,
if all possible objections must
be first overcome."*

Samuel Johnson

March 6

*Our world has changed over
the years because new ideas
were acted upon.
People may not have had all
the answers, but as they
began to take action,
the answers became clear!*

"It's a funny thing about life;
if you refuse to accept anything
but the best, you very often get it."
W. Somerset Maugham

You alone determine what you will accept from life, not your spouse, friend, mother, father, or employer. If you expect no more and do no more to better your life, then mediocrity is what you will have. But if you are determined to do more, to be more, then you will get more. You see, it all depends on what you are willing to accept.

We make our life whatever we want simply by the choices we make. We are all responsible for our own lives. Some people relinquish responsibility by blaming everyone and everything for their failures, lack of income, or large debts.

There are many stories of people who found themselves in desperate situations, but they were unwilling to accept the situation as permanent. Instead, they did more and became more. What are you willing to accept in your life?

Accept only the best!

MARCH 8

*"We become what we think
about all day long."*
Ralph Waldo Emerson

MARCH 9

*"Life will always be to a large
extent what we ourselves make it."*
Samuel Smiles

MARCH 10

"Prosperity is a great teacher;
adversity a greater."

William Hazlitt

We can always learn more from challenging times than from good times.

Adversity is the catalyst that forces us to stretch. It propels us to find solutions to problems we never would have considered if not for adversity.

Adversity can provide the fuel that sparks new strengths we didn't realize we had within us.

How we cope with adversity is also a learning experience. There are times in all of our lives where we have handled adversity well, and times where we have not.

Next time adversity strikes, remember, you can use it to your advantage by learning from it.

MARCH 11

"One who gains strength
by overcoming obstacles
possesses the only strength
which can overcome adversity."
Albert Schweitzer

MARCH 12

"Adversity has the effect of
eliciting talents, which in
prosperous circumstances
would have lain dormant."
Horace

March 13

*"Great minds have purposes,
others have wishes."*
Washington Irving

We all have great minds. What makes a difference is whether or not we use the full capability of our mind.

Those who have a *"purpose"* are active in setting goals and constantly working towards them.

Those who simply *"wish"*, have no specific goals for themselves; they just go day to day allowing someone else to set their direction. Wishing for something occupies the mind but leaves the bank empty.

Use your *"great mind"*, and set goals to achieve your purpose. Wishing is just as ineffective as worrying — neither accomplishes anything. Next time you find yourself wishing for something, remind yourself that wishing won't move you forward, but setting goals and taking action will!

March 14

*"A man will sometimes devote
all his life to the development
of one part of his body —
the wishbone."*

Robert Frost

March 15

*"Many of us spend half our time
wishing for things we could have
if we didn't spend half our time
wishing."*

Alexander Woollcott

MARCH 16

Eliminate time wasters by adopting a vacation attitude!

I get more done in the week before I go on vacation than I do in the previous month.

Why?

Because I am very focused. I know exactly what must be accomplished before I feel comfortable leaving for vacation.

Why can't we have this attitude everyday? The reason is that we know we will be there tomorrow, and we allow *"time wasters"* to creep into our day and steal our time. We can be very busy but achieve few results.

We need to develop a *"vacation attitude"* every day by being focused on what we need to accomplish by the end of each day. By focusing on results, we are spending our time wisely. By developing this attitude, we dramatically improve our performance, our productivity and our value to others.

MARCH 17

*"Never confuse motion
with action."*
    Benjamin Franklin

MARCH 18

*"It is not enough to be busy;
so are the ants.
The question is:
What are we busy about?"*
    Henry David Thoreau

MARCH 19

"There is no security on this earth;
there is only opportunity."
General Douglas MacArthur

Some people prefer to be secure rather than take a risk to pursue an opportunity. Too many people stay in secure jobs they hate, doing what they've always done. This often leads to depression, bitter feelings, or illness.

Some people insist in living in conditions they could improve. Why? Because the security of knowing what to expect, even though unrewarding, is more comforting than venturing into the unknown. For them, it is better to miss an opportunity than to risk potential ridicule from their friends. They prefer to cling to their view of security rather than take a chance, or seize an opportunity.

It is important to understand there is truly no security in anything. Your security results from the opportunities that you seize.

55

MARCH 20

"Too many people are thinking
of security instead of opportunity.
They seem more afraid
of life than death."
James F. Byrnes

MARCH 21

"Far better it is to dare mighty
things, to win glorious triumphs,
even though checkered by failure,
than to rank with those poor
spirits who neither enjoy much
nor suffer much because they
live in the grey twilight that
knows neither victory nor defeat."
Theodore Roosevelt

MARCH 22

*"The optimist sees the rose and
not its thorns;
the pessimist stares at the thorns,
oblivious to the rose."*

Kahlil Gibran

Do you see roses or do you see thorns? Only you can change your focus. For every negative there is a positive. Sometimes, we have to search hard for it, but it is there!

How do you see life's obstacles? Obstacles are not insurmountable barriers. They are, instead, your stepping stones. Let obstacles be your launching point to propel you to gain new experiences, personal growth, and well earned success. By viewing obstacles as necessary stepping stones, you will welcome them and not avoid them.

We have a choice in every situation we face. We can stare at the thorns, and feel sorry for ourselves, or we can see the positive. People experience continuous misery in their lives because they focus only on the thorns and completely miss the roses.

March 23

"The block of granite which
was an obstacle in the
pathway of the weak
becomes a stepping-stone
in the pathway of the strong."
Thomas Carlyle

March 24

The Hare and the Hound

"A Hound chased a Hare, but after
a long run, gave up the chase.
A goat seeing him stop, mocked
him, saying 'The little one is the
best runner of the two.'
The Hound replied, 'You do not see
the difference between us:
I was only running for dinner, but
he for his life'."
Aesop

*Do not be discouraged if your
plans do not succeed the first time.
No one learns to walk by taking
only one step!*

When faced with failure, reflect on this
Japanese proverb: "Fall seven times,
stand up eight." As long as you keep
getting up, you are not failing.

Those who learn how to overcome failure
become stronger. Let's face it, we are all
confronted with failure. The difference is
how we deal with it.

Some people use failure as an excuse to
give up, to become bitter, or cynical. Other
people look at failure as an opportunity to
revisit past decisions and to devise new
strategies.

Thousands of successful people did not
achieve success on their first try, but they
were not discouraged. They picked
themselves up and went back at it with an
even stronger, single minded tenacity to
achieve their goal.

MARCH 26

*"A problem is a chance
for you to do your best."*
Duke Ellington

MARCH 27

*"Difficulties strengthen the mind,
as well as labor does the body."*
Seneca

MARCH 28

"Success seems to be largely
a matter of hanging on after
others have let go."
William Feather

Some of the significant differences between winning and losing are:

Hanging on, persevering.	=	**Winning**
Letting go, giving up easily.	=	**Losing**
Accepting responsibility for your actions.	=	**Winning**
Always having an excuse for your actions.	=	**Losing**
Taking the initiative.	=	**Winning**
Waiting to be told what to do.	=	**Losing**
Knowing what you want and setting goals to achieve it.	=	**Winning**
Wishing for things, but taking no action.	=	**Losing**
Seeing the big picture, and setting your goals accordingly.	=	**Winning**
Seeing only where you are today.	=	**Losing**

Adopt a WINNING attitude!

March 29

*"The gent who wakes up
and finds himself a success
hasn't been asleep."*
Wilson Mizner

March 30

*"Success usually comes to
those who are too busy
to be looking for it."*
Henry David Thoreau

*"Once there were 3 bricklayers.
Each one of them was asked what
they were doing.*

*The first man answered gruffly,
'I'm laying bricks.'
The second man replied,
'I'm putting up a wall.'
But the third man said
enthusiastically and with pride,
'I'm building a cathedral'."*

Author Unknown

This story clearly reveals two secrets of success:

1. *ATTITUDE.*
Your attitude towards whatever you are doing determines your ultimate level of success.

2. *ABILITY TO SEE THE BIGGER PICTURE.*
Being able to see the end result, rather than just the task, eliminates obstacles, focuses your energy, and provides motivation to excel.

"A man can fail many times, but he isn't a failure until he begins to blame somebody else."

John Burrough

April

APRIL 1

"A man who trims himself to suit everybody will soon whittle himself away."

Charles M. Schwab

The person you have to account to is you. You should never try to mold yourself to meet anyone else's desires, or views.

Attempting to please everyone in your life will only cause internal conflict, a sure formula for failure. As well, you may easily find yourself working on their dreams and not your own.

As you work to achieve your goals, some people will criticize you. Their criticism, however, may be no more than jealousy. Don't let someone else's opinions stop you.

Rather than focusing your energy on trying to become what other people want, decide on who you want to become. Focus your energy on achieving your own wants and desires.

APRIL 2

"To escape criticism —
do nothing,
say nothing,
be nothing."

Elbert Hubbard

APRIL 3

"Whatever you do,
you need courage.
Whatever course you decide upon,
there is always someone to tell you
that you are wrong.
There are always difficulties
arising that tempt you to believe
your critics are right."

Ralph Waldo Emerson

"It's amazing what ordinary people
can do if they set out without
preconceived notions."
Charles F. Kettering

Think of young children just starting to learn how to walk. Children have no preconceived notion that they cannot walk on their first few attempts. Imagine what would happen if we said, "Don't try to walk, you will fall". Sounds silly doesn't it?

As adults, though, we often send ourselves failure messages due to our preconceived notions. We don't take advantage of opportunities because we're afraid we won't succeed.

People who say, "I'd do it but I don't have the time", or "I don't have the money", are only making excuses. What they really don't have is determination.

Imagine how different our lives would be if we were to rid our minds of thoughts of failure or lame excuses, and, instead, attempted things with an "I will succeed" conviction. We need to re-develop the same basic instinct children have when they first attempt to walk!

APRIL 5

A determined person will do more with a pen and paper, than a lazy person will accomplish with a personal computer.

APRIL 6

"People of mediocre ability sometimes achieve outstanding success because they don't know when to quit. Most men succeed because they are determined to."
George Allen

*"Those who dream by day
are cognizant of many things
which escape those who
dream only by night."*
Edgar Allan Poe

Many successes can be attributed to
those who dream. Dreaming is a gift
where you can see things not as they are,
but as they could be.

People who never dream, or never set
goals, let life go by day by day letting
others determine their destiny.

Without dreams, you don't set goals; you
are forced to accept what you have today.

As children, we had lots of dreams. When
we get older, some of us lose our dreams
and our ambitions, and are content to
accept mediocrity.

Everything that has ever been
accomplished, every skyscraper, every
bridge, every invention, every medical
breakthrough, all started with a dream!

APRIL 8

*"If you have built castles in the air,
your work need not be lost; that is
where they should be.
Now put the foundations under
them."*

Henry David Thoreau

APRIL 9

*"Hold fast to dreams,
for if dreams die,
life is a broken winged bird
that cannot fly."*

Langston Hughes

APRIL 10

"Try to do unto others as you
would have them do to you,
and do not be discouraged
if they fail sometimes.
It is much better that they should
fail than that you should."
Charles Dickens

Dickens' quote is one of my all time
favourites. If we all lived our lives
putting this attitude at the forefront of our
thoughts, we would not be so quick to give
up on people. Sometimes, though, when
we treat people as we want to be treated,
they turn around and treat us badly. How
often do we immediately change our
feelings and respond with the same kind of
negative treatment?

We never know what tomorrow may
bring. The people we meet today may have
a dramatic influence on our lives
tomorrow.

It really changes your feelings, and more
importantly, your actions, when you adopt
the attitude that "it is better that they fail
than me"!

APRIL 11

A SHORT COURSE IN HUMAN RELATIONS

"The 6 most important words: I ADMIT THAT I WAS WRONG. *The 5 most important words:* YOU DID A GREAT JOB! *The 4 most important words:* WHAT DO YOU THINK? *The 3 most important words:* COULD YOU PLEASE. *The 2 most important words:* THANK YOU! *The <u>most</u> important word:* WE. *The <u>least</u> important word:* I.*"*

Author Unknown

APRIL 12

"Always be nice to people on the way up; because you'll meet the same people on the way down."

Wilson Mizner

*"Man cannot discover new oceans
unless he has the courage to lose
sight of the shore."*
Andre Gide

To achieve our goals, we must be
willing to have the courage that takes
us beyond familiar territory, familiar
actions, or familiar skills.

To *"discover new oceans"* means to
relinquish familiar things that currently
give us comfort and security.

We must be willing to stretch by having
the courage to try things that we have
never done before. It may require us to
improve our knowledge or to learn new
skills.

The first time we do anything new, we
may be afraid of failing. But we must have
the courage to master fear.

Although, thousands of people are afraid
of failing, they find the courage to counter
their fears by taking action.

APRIL 14

"All our dreams can come true —
if we have the courage to
pursue them."
Walt Disney

APRIL 15

"Life shrinks or expands in
proportion to one's courage."
Anais Nin

*Life gives us a choice of
where we sit —
in the passenger's or
the driver's seat!*

Y ou determine what road you will
travel, when you will turn, when you
will stop, how fast or how slow you will
go.

Some people sit in the passenger's seat of
life and never learn how to drive. They let
other people determine when, where, how
fast or slow they will go. They don't set
goals.

Setting goals provides you with a preferred
path to follow. Goals determine what road
you will go down, when you will turn and
when you will stop. Putting a time frame
on the accomplishment of your goals
determines how fast, or how slow you go.

**Sit in the driver's seat,
set your own goals and
determine where you will go!**

APRIL 17

*"If you do not sow in the spring
you will not reap in the autumn."*

Irish Proverb

APRIL 18

"You will reap what you sow."

Russian Proverb

APRIL 19

*"Things may come to those
who wait, but only the things
left by those who hustle."*
Abraham Lincoln

How often have we heard about a new
product, or a new way of doing
something, and it was exactly what we had
already thought about. Someone else
received credit for it because they took the
action and did it.

We can spend hours, days, months, even
years, thinking or talking about something
we want to accomplish. But, nothing
happens until we take action!

People have lots of ideas, yet they never
take a step towards implementation. They
think it can't be done, or that it would take
too much work, or they listen to other
people who tell them it won't work.

Has someone ever voiced an idea you've
been thinking about, and everyone thought
it was great?

Don't be left behind
take action on your ideas!

APRIL 20

"The world is moving so fast these days that the man who says it can't be done is generally interrupted by someone doing it."
Elbert Hubbard

APRIL 21

"You will never plough a field if you only turn it over in your mind."
Irish Proverb

APRIL 22

"Seize the day, and put the least possible trust in tomorrow."

Horace

Who says tomorrow will bring success, happiness or wealth?

A lot of us live our lives by counting on what we will accomplish tomorrow.

Do you wish your life away by waiting for tomorrow?

When I was younger, I couldn't wait for that one thing that was going to happen tomorrow. My Dad used to tell me I was wishing my life away.

We all know, as a certainty, our days are numbered. We also never know when our number will come up. Rather than putting off until tomorrow, take action and do the things you want to accomplish today.

**Make every day count as if
there is no tomorrow!**

APRIL 23

"Live as you will have wished to have lived when you are dying."
Christian F. Gellert

APRIL 24

"First *I was dying to finish high school and start college.*
And then *I was dying to finish college and start working.*
And then *I was dying to marry and have children.*
And then *I was dying for my children to grow old enough for school so I could return to work.*
And then *I was dying to retire.*
And now,
I AM dying — and suddenly I realize
I forgot to live."
Author Unknown

APRIL 25

*"Tact is the art of building a fire
under people without
making their blood boil."*
Franklin P. Jones

In relating to people, *"tact"* is one skill,
when mastered, allows us to
communicate in a manner that encourages
people to make positive contributions.

We've all heard the saying, "It's not what
you say, it is how you say it". There are
times when we need to say something
someone else needs to hear. How we say it
determines whether or not they listen.
How?

First, look at the situation from the other
person's point of view. Secondly, expand
on the explanation so they receive all the
information they need to help them see the
whole picture.

We have to interact with people in all areas
of our life. "How to Win Friends &
Influence People" by Dale Carnegie offers
good suggestions on how to deal more
effectively with people.

81

APRIL 26

"If there is any one secret
of success, it lies in the
ability to get the other person's
point of view and see things from
that person's angle as well as
from your own."

Henry Ford

APRIL 27

"The most important single
ingredient in the formula of
success is knowing how to
get along with people."

Theodore Roosevelt

*"The fellow who doesn't need a
boss is often selected to be one."*
Christopher Morley

Do you need someone to tell you what
to do, when to do it, and how to do it?
Or, are you the type of person who takes
the initiative? The people who reap the
rewards are those who go beyond their
assigned duties.

Many people don't understand why they
are by-passed for promotions. If they
stopped and objectively looked at the
differences between themselves and the
person who got the promotion, they would
see why.

Some people mentally quit their job years
ago, but their body still goes to work every
day. These type of people are quite willing
to let others do their work for them.
However, in the end, they are the ones
who usually suffer.

Learn what you need to by taking the
initiative, do things without being told,
have a positive attitude, and be reliable.
These personal attributes can readily assist
you in a successful career.

APRIL 29

"People who never do any
more than they get paid for,
never get paid for any
more than they do."
                                    Elbert Hubbard

APRIL 30

"The world is full of willing people;
some willing to work,
the rest willing to let them."
                                    Robert Frost

May

MAY 1

"Throughout the centuries there were men who took first steps down new roads, armed with nothing but their vision."
Ayn Rand

What is your vision of the future? To have a vision for your life is to see where you could be, not where you are now. Great leaders move people not by what they see today, but by what they see as the future.

Your vision may result in travelling down a different road than your friends.

Many corporations have clearly defined "vision" statements. These statements allow the employees, and shareholders, to see where the company wants to go, and what it wants to achieve.

Do you know what you want, and where you are going? A vision allows you to look forward to the future with positive expectations for yourself.

85

MAY 2

*"Vision is the art of
seeing things invisible."*
Jonathan Swift

MAY 3

*"If you want to succeed you
should strike out on new paths
rather than travel the worn paths
of accepted success."*
John D. Rockefeller, Jr.

MAY 4

*"Where there is a will,
there is a way."*
English Proverb

If you have the determination, the desire,
and the *will*, you'll find a way to achieve
your greatest desires. Your *will* determines
the shape of your life. It determines your
level of commitment to keep going, it
allows you to see the finish line because
you believe that you will reach it.

But, if your willpower is feeble, or your
determination is unsteady, your chances
for accomplishment are slim. You may find
yourself using the excuse that it is
impossible.

With a powerful will, you can find ways to
achieve your goals, and overcome
challenges. When you concentrate on your
goals and ignore daily distractions, you
will succeed. You must have the necessary
discipline to reach your goal.

**If you have the "WILL",
the "WAY" will unmask itself!**

MAY 5

"He who has a firm will,
molds the world to himself."
Goethe

MAY 6

"Nothing is impossible;
there are ways that lead to
everything, and
if we had sufficient will
we should always have
sufficient means.
It is often merely for an excuse
that we say things are
impossible."
Francois La Rochefoucauld

*"Reflect on your present blessings,
of which every man has many,
not on your past misfortunes,
of which all men have some."*

Charles Dickens

We all have many blessings. If you made a list of all the things you could be thankful for, the list would undoubtedly be longer than your misfortunes.

Accept whatever your misfortune is and move on. There are some things over which you have no control, and to dwell on them serves no useful purpose. Adopting the *"poor me"* attitude gives no promise and offers no gain.

A lot of the things we take for granted would be considered a blessing by someone in less fortunate circumstances. Take our health care system, for example. It is only a dream for millions of other people in the world, yet it's something we take for granted.

When you think of life, think first about the blessings you have. Don't focus on misfortunes, for they are but a faint shadow.

MAY 8

*"You cannot prevent the bird of
sorrow from flying over your head,
but you can prevent it from
building nests in your hair."*
Chinese Proverb

MAY 9

*"The longer we dwell on our
misfortunes, the greater their
power to harm us."*
Voltaire

MAY 10

"One's mind,
once stretched by a new idea,
never regains its original
dimensions."
Oliver Wendell Holmes

There are numerous examples of the above theme; here is a small sampling:

- the automobile, once, was just an idea.
- the microwave, once, was just an idea.
- the computer, once, was just an idea.
- the TV, once, was just an idea.
- the telephone, once, was just an idea.
- the Internet, once, was just an idea.

Today, most of us have some of the above conveniences, and would find it hard to imagine life without them. An idea can "stretch" your mind with the potential of influencing the lives of thousands of people.

Let every invention around you
be your motivation,
as they were once all just ideas!

MAY 11

*"Ideas won't keep;
something must be done
about them."*
Alfred North Whitehead

MAY 12

*"The man with a new idea is a
crank until the idea succeeds."*
Mark Twain

"Laughter is the sun that drives winter from the human face."

Victor Hugo

How serious life would be without laughter.

- Laughter takes away the stresses of the day.
- Laughter is contagious, it spreads like ripples in the water and makes everyone feel better.
- It makes life's problems a little less serious and a lot more bearable.
- Laughter has been found to help people recover from illness.
- Laughter can help us see a situation from a different perspective.

To go through a day without laughing makes us older than our time. It takes less energy to smile than it does to frown.

Did you know that it takes 72 muscles to frown, and it only takes 14 muscles to smile!

MAY 14

*"A person without a sense of
humor is like
a wagon without springs —
jolted by every pebble in the road."*
Henry Ward Beecher

MAY 15

*"The most wasted of all days
is one without laughter."*
e. e. cummings

MAY 16

*"Time is the most valuable thing
a man can spend."*

Diogenes Laertius

What is the one thing we all have in common?

No matter who we are, what we do, where we live, or how much money we have, each of us has 24 hours in every day. What makes us different from each other is how we use our time.

What value do you place on your time? Would you throw a hundred dollar bill to the wind or out of a window? I doubt it! Yet, some people adopt this kind of attitude about their time.

Some people sleep their time away. Do you realize that if you get up just 30 minutes earlier every day for one year, you would have an additional 182 hours a year to devote to a worthwhile project.

Don't squander your time foolishly. To understand the value of time is to realize that once it is gone, you never get it back!

MAY 17

*"I wish I could stand
on a busy corner,
hat in hand,
and beg people
to throw me all their
wasted hours."*
Bernard Berenson

MAY 18

*"Lost wealth may be
replaced by industry,
lost knowledge by study,
lost health by
temperance or medicine,
but lost time is gone forever."*
Samuel Smiles

MAY 19

*"I can't change the direction of the
wind, but I can adjust my sails to
always reach my destination."*
Jimmy Dean

A friend of mine had a terrible
childhood. He was one of five
children, his father was an alcoholic and
died very young, and his mother was
unable to support the family.
Unfortunately, the children were separated
and placed in foster homes. My friend
dropped out of school and did nothing to
further himself even though opportunities
were available to him. He eventually went
through a divorce. My friend's brother,
although experiencing the same childhood,
educated himself and obtained a job as a
welder. He has a close family and a
wonderful home.

Both brothers give a similar answer when
asked why their lives turned out the way
they did:
"You'd turn out this way too, if you had a
childhood like mine."

**Neither one of the brothers could change
his past, but one of them adjusted his sail!**

MAY 20

*"Life consists not in holding
good cards but in playing those
you hold well."*

Josh Billings

MAY 21

*"I studied the lives of
great men and famous women,
and I found that the men and
women who got to the top were
those who did the jobs they had
in hand, with everything they had
of energy and enthusiasm and
hard work."*

Harry S. Truman

MAY 22

*"If we all did the things we are
capable of doing, we would
literally astound ourselves."*
Thomas A. Edison

Ask yourself, what stops you from doing all you are capable of doing? All too often, we put limits on ourselves by doubting our own abilities, and not confronting our fears.

Self-limiting beliefs actually stop us from achieving great success. These beliefs may be ones we grew up with, such as: "I'm not smart enough", or "I don't have the right education".

We also place limits on ourselves because of the fear of failure. Fear paralyzes far too many people from achieving their dreams. It is a conscious choice to let fear control you. You can master your fears, but first you must make a commitment to take action.

The vast majority of successful people are ordinary people. What is extraordinary about them is how strongly they believed in themselves.

MAY 23

*"We gain strength, and courage,
and confidence by each experience
in which we really stop to
look fear in the face...
we must do that which we think
we cannot."*

Eleanor Roosevelt

MAY 24

*"Nothing is so much
to be feared as fear."*

Henry David Thoreau

*See the possibilities in
all situations!*

When all seems to be doom and
gloom, there are still positive
possibilities; you just have to look for
them. Too often, we only see the negatives.

Learn to look at every difficult situation as
a present; the gift within is the possibilities
it holds.

For example, a couple buys a rundown
house. They see the house as it could be,
not as it is. What they see is the
"possibility".

Or, you may lose your job. The
"possibility" is you can focus your full
energy on changing careers, or finding a
job in an area you've always wanted.

If you focus on the possible when you
experience difficult situations you can
positively change your outlook, reduce
your stress, and concentrate on achieving
things that otherwise may not have been
possible.

MAY 26

*"In the middle of difficulty
lies opportunity."*

Albert Einstein

MAY 27

*"I always tried to turn every
disaster into an opportunity."*

John D. Rockefeller, Jr.

MAY 28

*"The creation of a thousand
forests is in one acorn."*
Ralph Waldo Emerson

How many times have you felt
overwhelmed by the sheer size of a
problem, task, or a goal?

For most people, the hardest part in
moving forward is taking that first step.
You could end up creating *"a thousand
forests"*, but nothing will be achieved until
you take that first step. The results of doing
that *"one"* act could dramatically influence
the lives of thousands of people.

Take, for example, the quest to put a man
on the moon. Was it a little problem?
Obviously not. How was it accomplished?
By taking that first step, then another,
then ...

You may be inspired to take action by
knowing that many years ago the saying,
"reach for the stars", was taken very
seriously by only a few. This is especially
noteworthy when most people said it was
impossible!

MAY 29

*"The man who removes a mountain
begins by carrying away
small stones."*

Chinese Proverb

MAY 30

*"Nothing is particularly hard
if you divide it into small jobs."*

Henry Ford

*"The reason why so few people
are agreeable in conversation is
that each is thinking more about
what he intends to say than
about what others are saying,
and we never listen when
we are eager to speak."*
Francois La Rochefoucauld

A bove all others, listening is the most important skill in communication.

At a seminar I attended, the instructor asked, "do you **hear,** or do you **listen**?" The point is that a lot of people hear words but do not pay close attention to the intent of the message.

To effectively listen:
- maintain eye contact with the person;
- don't jump to conclusions, let people finish what they are saying;
- listen for changes in voice tone;
- watch the person's body language;
- ask questions to ensure you understand correctly.

Listen, don't just hear!

"Just don't give up trying to do what you really want to do. Where there is love and inspiration, I don't think you can go wrong."
Ella Fitzgerald

June

JUNE 1

*"If you enjoy what you do,
you'll never work another
day in your life."*

Confucius

If you love what you do, it will not seem like work. The secret to success is to find a job that you love, and truly, you will never work another day in your life.

Too often, we settle for a job that we don't enjoy. A lot of people work with only the thought of Friday in their minds; the weekend is their most treasured escape. If you truly love what you do, then you will find personal reward and happiness in each and every day, not just on weekends. Monday to Friday are days of your life, live them.

As I read about successful people, two characteristics keep appearing:
1. they love what they do;
2. they have extraordinary drive.

What do you really enjoy doing?
Once you find it,
you will find extraordinary drive also!

June 2

*"Some men go through a forest
and see no firewood."*
English Proverb

June 3

*"You have to know what
you want to get it."*
Gertrude Stein

JUNE 4

*"I haven't failed. I've found
10,000 ways that don't work."*
Thomas A. Edison

If we all had Edison's attitude, there
would be a lot more recorded successes
in this world.

Let your attitude reflect the belief that an
event called "failure" is a means that
brings you one step closer to success. When
you fail, you have learned, by the process
of elimination, one more way that won't
work. Your next attempt should
incorporate all that you have learned,
bringing you one step closer to success.

Look at the difference in attitude:
A. I found 10,000 things that didn't work,
or,
B. I failed in 10,000 attempts.

When you read the attitude reflected in *B*,
it demoralizes you and damages your
self-image; the attitude reflected in *A*
motivates you.

Remember Edison's attitude and try to
look at life with an *"A"*attitude!

JUNE 5

*"Men succeed when they realize
that their failures are the
preparation for their victories."*
Ralph Waldo Emerson

JUNE 6

*"Some defeats are only
installments to victory."*
Jacob A. Riis

JUNE 7

*"It is better to be prepared
for an opportunity and
not have one than to have an
opportunity and not be prepared."*
Whitney Young Jr.

Continuous learning prepares you to take advantage of opportunities.

Setting a goal of continuous learning is the first step in being prepared to see an opportunity. The process of learning both stimulates and challenges your mind, and increases your capacity to see things in a new and different light.

You cannot expect to attain success if you are not prepared. Life has a habit of giving back rewards in proportion to the effort we expend. If you put in little effort and expect big returns, you will be deeply disappointed. You don't get apples by planting lemon seeds.

Once an opportunity is identified, action must be taken. As part of your preparation to take full advantage of opportunities, make continuous learning a way of life.

111

JUNE 8

*"By failing to prepare you
are preparing to fail."*
Benjamin Franklin

JUNE 9

*"A cynic is not merely one who
reads bitter lessons from the past;
he is one who is prematurely
disappointed in the future."*
Sydney J. Harris

JUNE 10

"Thought is action in rehearsal."
Sigmund Freud

What we think is only a rehearsal.

The play begins once we take action. We can think and think about things for a long time, but if we don't take action, our thinking is only a rehearsal.

The same applies to talking. It is easy to talk about what we are going to do, but it doesn't mean anything until we take action and make it happen.

What is it you would like to achieve? *Think* about what it is you want. Then, set realistic goals by asking yourself whether your goals are consistent with your own values? *Communicate* your goal. Write it down. Verbally share it with someone you trust and who will support you. Then, take *action!* Start working toward your goals today.

Don't let your ideas and goals be just a rehearsal. Take action and let them be the play of your life!

JUNE 11

"Thought is the blossom;
language the bud;
action the fruit behind."
Ralph Waldo Emerson

JUNE 12

"The time for action is now.
It's never too late to do something."
Carl Sandburg

114

JUNE 13

Teaching allows you to share your wealth while at the same time increasing your own wealth.

When you teach, you are also clarifying what you have learned.

There are times when we feel our knowledge isn't strong enough to teach someone else. Thorough subject preparation beforehand will not only strengthen your own knowledge, but will greatly increase your comfort level in teaching others.

All of us have gained knowledge through years of experience and education in various areas. The ability and willingness to impart onto others that same knowledge is a gift. We should always use it to help those around us.

Pass on your knowledge, and your reward will be twofold:
1. your own understanding will increase,
2. you will have made a significant contribution in helping others gain valuable knowledge!

June 14

"To teach is to learn twice."
Joseph Joubert

June 15

"He who opens a school door,
closes a prison door."
Victor Hugo

*"People who fly into a rage
always make a bad landing."*
Will Rogers

One of the best lessons you can learn in life is to master how to remain calm. Don't let challenges upset you.

I have worked with people who overreact to situations and get easily ruffled about the most trivial issues. Unfortunately, these people don't focus on solutions. They only focus on the problem, which makes a solution much harder to find.

When you are angry, the best thing to do is to say nothing. Another good technique is to stop and ask yourself, *"Is it really important?"* or *"Does it really matter?"* You may find this technique changes your perception, allowing you to react with clearer thought and much less personal emotion.

It is important to understand that you are the master controller of your reactions, no matter what the circumstances.

JUNE 17

"Nothing gives one person so much advantage over another as to remain always cool and unruffled under all circumstances."
Thomas Jefferson

JUNE 18

"The best time for you to hold your tongue is the time you feel you must say something or bust."
Josh Billings

"Advice is like snow;
the softer it falls,
the longer it dwells upon, and
the deeper it sinks into the mind."
Samuel Taylor

Be sure that you are not forceful, or do not put another person down when you are giving advice.

Before you offer advice try and understand the situation from their point of view.

Always try to identify the benefits of your advice to the other person.

On the other hand, it may be that the best advice is to give no advice. I'm sure there are many situations where people look to you for guidance. Occasionally, though, the best "advice" is to ask them to decide on their own, and to take action based on their own decision.

Always be aware of the advice you offer by asking yourself whether your own personal behavior reflects your words.

June 20

"The true secret of giving advice is,
after you have honestly given it,
to be perfectly indifferent
whether it is taken or not, and
never persist in trying to
set people right."

Hannah W. Smith

June 21

"He that gives good advice,
builds with one hand;
he that gives good counsel,
and example, builds with both;
but he that gives good admonition
and bad example,
builds with one hand and pulls
down with the other."

Francis Bacon

JUNE 22

We are all infectious.
What matters is what type of
infectious person we are.

Have you ever noticed that some people's laughter is infectious; it makes you laugh. The average child laughs at least 100 - 200 times a day. But, the average adult **only** laughs 10 to 15 times a day!

One of your most valuable assets is a good sense of humor. In general, humorous people are fun to be with, have less stress and a healthier outlook on life.

Other people possess so much enthusiasm it rubs off on those around them.

There are also people who have such a positive outlook on life that you find talking with them helps you to be positive. And, there are those who are so motivated to excel they actually inspire others!

On the other hand, some people are so depressing, so negative, and so cynical, they only bring you down.

Which type of infectious person are you?

June 23

"Good humor is one of the
best articles of dress one
can wear in society."
William Thackeray

June 24

"Good nature is worth
more than knowledge,
more than money,
more than honour,
to the persons who possess it."
Henry Ward Beecher

*"Every seed knows its time —
all in good time."*

Russian Proverb

A plant does not immediately spring to life after you sow the seed.

Unfortunately, we often assume that our life will instantly change once we have an idea, or once we begin to work on a project or plan. All too often, we become far too impatient.

When we set goals, we must remember that action steps are the seeds that will lead us toward the accomplishment of our goal.

Having patience will allow you to persevere in reaching your goals, and not be discouraged by any setbacks or rejections.

Seeds must be nourished and given time to flourish. Don't be discouraged if you do not meet with immediate success. Remember, a seed does not bloom overnight.

June 26

*"Genius is nothing but
a greater aptitude for patience."*
George L. Buffon

June 27

*"Little drops of water
wear down big stones."*
Russian Proverb

JUNE 28

*Be thankful for change.
It has made our lives easier!*

When we compare the standard of living we enjoy today with that of the early 1900s, it should make us realize how lucky we are.

Although we still work hard, we work fewer hours. A farmer in the early 1900s easily worked 12 to 14 hours a day, six days a week.

Travelling is also a lot easier and faster. We can fly across the country and arrive the same day; during the early 1900s, this was impossible.

Communication today is unlike anything ever dreamed of in the early 1900s, with our computer modems, phones, and faxes.

All the modern conveniences we enjoy today are symbols that change means convenience, advancement, and development!

JUNE 29

*"Progress is impossible without
change, and those who
cannot change their minds
cannot change anything."*
George Bernard Shaw

JUNE 30

*"When one door closes another
door opens; but we so often look
so long and so regretfully upon
the closed door, that we do not
see the ones which open for us."*
Alexander Graham Bell

July

JULY 1

*"Life is not the way it is supposed
to be. It is the way it is.
The way you cope with it is what
makes the difference."*
Virginia Satir

How you cope with life is determined
by your mental attitude. How you
view any situation depends on your beliefs
and your values.

How you cope with challenges can
strengthen or weaken you. Some people
have faced numerous challenges in their
lives, yet maintained a positive outlook.

Reinforce your coping mechanisms by:
- viewing change as an opportunity, not
  as a threat,
- finding a positive benefit in your
  challenges,
- discussing the situation with a friend,
- taking action and not procrastinating,
- taking time to laugh,
and, above all,
- keeping things in perspective!

July 2

"No life is so hard that one can't make it easier by the way one accepts it."

Ellen Glasgow

July 3

"The highest reward for a person's toil is not what he gets for it, but what he becomes by it."

John Ruskin

July 4

"Imagination is more important than knowledge."

Albert Einstein

Imagination must come before knowledge.

As children, we have lots of imagination, but as we grow older, we come to believe knowledge is more important.

Imagination allows you to see things in a non-traditional, non-restrictive manner. Your imagination is your picture of what tomorrow may bring.

What about the first person who imagined a plane? The only thing that occupied the skies then were birds. It sounded absurd to think that someone could actually build a machine that would allow people to fly! Yet, Orville and Wilbur Wright's imagination saw that plane. Today, not being able to fly sounds even more absurd.

Use all of your knowledge and resources to turn things imagined, into reality.

July 5

"*Your imagination is your preview
of life's coming attractions.*"
Albert Einstein

July 6

"*Anything one man can imagine,
other men can make real.*"
Jules Verne

Fix the problem,
not the blame!

Think how much time and emotion we
expend when we try to place blame
for something that didn't work, or try to
decide where the fault lies.

Rather than criticizing others, spend your
time and energy on solving the problem.

Spending time finding fault does not solve
any problem, it only monopolizes your
time. If your focus is to find fault, you will
only end up with a lot more people
spending unproductive time covering their
tracks. If anything goes wrong, you can be
assured they will not be found at fault; this
is very ineffective.

Fixing the problem means that you are
utilizing your personal resources to work
in a more constructive and positive way.

Fixing the problem, rather than fixing the
blame, also sets a positive example for
others to follow!

JULY 8

*"Don't find fault,
find a remedy."*
Henry Ford

JULY 9

*"If you are able to state a
problem, it can be solved."*
Edwin H. Land

By being persistent, you will find that failure doesn't last, as failure cannot cope with persistence!

Everyone meets failure in their journey through life. To overcome failure, you need to concentrate and focus your energy on your goal. If you don't succeed the first time, try another way.

We are easily distracted or side-tracked by working on areas that bear no relation to our goal. Keep your goal focused in your mind at all times.

Put your energy and effort into completing tasks that move you closer to your goal. Even if you set aside only 30 minutes a day, you are being persistent and consistently moving closer and closer to your goal.

Ask yourself if you have been defeated by your own lack of persistence without realizing it. Step back and take a hard look at how persistent you have really been.

July 11

"When you get into a tight
place and everything goes
against you 'till it seems
as though you could not hold
on a minute longer,
never give up then,
for that is just the place
and time that the tide will turn."
Harriet Beecher Stowe

July 12

"Consider the postage stamp:
its usefulness consists in the
ability to stick to one thing
till it gets there."
Josh Billings

134

*"There are no circumstances,
however unfortunate, that clever
people do not extract some
advantage from."*

Francois La Rochefoucauld

There are advantages and opportunities in all circumstances.

A story that reflects this is about a young divorced woman who had to support herself and her son. Bette Nesmith Graham obtained work as a typist, however her typing skills were poor! She could not afford to lose her job, yet the accuracy of her typing would not guarantee her job. She came up with the idea of using a waterbase paint to cover up her mistakes, which allowed her to type over them. Other typists started using her formula. Eventually, she sold her formula, "Liquid Paper", for millions of dollars to Gillette Corporation.

**Here was a person in an unfortunate
circumstance, but she was able to
gain advantage from it!**

July 14

"*Small opportunities are often the beginning of great enterprises.*"
Demosthenes

July 15

"*A wise man will make more opportunities than he finds.*"
Francis Bacon

Repeatedly, we attempt the impossible and try to change other people — but attempting this is a waste of time!

Think of a time when you tried to change a personal habit. As we have absolute control over how we think, you would assume changing a habit is easy. It is not.

Stop and consider how difficult it is for us to try and change other people when we have no control over their thoughts. You cannot change other people, you can only change yourself. If you want them to change, then you must change.

Whether it is the behaviour of a child, a boss, a co-worker, a friend, or a spouse you are the one who must change. You can change the way you express your feelings towards the behaviour. Or, you can change your reaction to the behaviour. In some cases, you may have to change by accepting the behaviour. The point is, you have control over you and that is the only person you can change.

July 17

*"Everyone thinks of changing
the world, but no one thinks
of changing himself."*

Leo Tolstoy

July 18

*Rather than wishing for change,
you first must be prepared to
change.*

JULY 19

"Books are the quietest and most
constant of friends;
they are the most accessible
and wisest of counselors,
and the most patient of teachers."
Charles W. Eliot

Everything that you need to know is in print. Books are printed on every subject imaginable. It doesn't matter what area you need to improve or what subject you want to research. A book is available.

The amount of information available today is almost overwhelming. Focus on the broad area you want to learn more about and narrow your research by subject matter — most libraries are now computerized to help in your search.

Lack of information cannot be used as an excuse for not furthering your knowledge. Every city has a public library full of appropriate books, no matter what your area of interest.

Far too often, people don't take the time to read a book or listen to an educational tape that would increase their knowledge. Don't use the excuse that you are too busy!

JULY 20

*"Education is not filling a bucket
but lighting a fire."*
William Butlet Yeats

JULY 21

*If you read every day for 30
minutes over the next year, it
would be equivalent to attending a
4 week course.*

*"No one can make you feel inferior
without your consent."*

Eleanor Roosevelt

You are responsible for every feeling you have. If you feel inferior to someone else, it is because of your own beliefs. How you react to situations is your personal choice. It is your decision, and yours alone, to determine the importance you give to any situation.

You can read all kinds of stories where people stuck to their beliefs even when they were told they would fail.

One of these stories is that of F. W. Woolworth. He was a **store clerk** who thought his boss should have a 10 cent sale to reduce his stock. His boss rejected the idea. The clerk *did not allow* his boss to make him feel inferior. Instead, he took his idea and put it into practice by opening his own store — "F. W. Woolworth Store". He then went on to open a chain of successful stores.

July 23

"If you look at life one way, there is always cause for alarm."
Elizabeth Bowen

July 24

"If you are distressed by anything external, the pain is not due to the thing itself but to your own estimate of it; and this you have the power to revoke at any moment."
Marcus Aurelius

*"Happiness is not the absence
of problems;
but the ability to deal with them."*
Jack Brown

The way we perceive our problems, and
the importance we give to them,
determines how we will deal with them.
Why?

Because the world is a reflection of our
mind. We can see a world full of problems,
or we can see a world filled with
challenges with the realization we have the
capacity to overcome them. We can let our
problems depress us, or we can accept life's
challenges and deal with them as they
occur.

We have the ability to determine our
happiness hour by hour and day by day,
through our thoughts and actions.

We make that choice every morning when
we get out of bed. We can choose to look
forward to the day, or we can choose to
moan and complain.

It's your choice!

July 26

"People are just about as happy as they make up their minds to be."
Abraham Lincoln

July 27

How you choose to react will determine your happiness and success!

"Don't forget until too late
that the business of life
is not business,
but living."
B. C. Forbes

Have you ever noticed the actions of someone who has had a heart attack. They change their work habits, exercise regularly, and allow more time for leisure.

The problem today is we get so caught up in our work that we don't allow ourselves time to relax. We don't allow time to get away from it all, and to do something totally different and enjoyable.

We all need to remember to maintain a balance between work and play. Our health is our most valued possession.

Maintain a good balance!
Your life depends on it!

July 29

*"A man too busy to take
care of his health is like a
mechanic too busy to
take care of his tools."*
Spanish Proverb

July 30

*"One today is worth
two tomorrows."*
Benjamin Franklin

JULY 31

*"I'd rather regret the things that I
have done than
the things that I have not done."*

Lucille Ball

One of my regrets is that I accepted a
position that involved a lot of
overnight travelling.

My co-workers warned me not to accept it
because my children were still young. I
thought being away would not pose any
problems because I only saw my children
for a brief period in the morning and for
one hour in the evening.

I took the job, but immediately started to
hate being away even for one night. I
ended up taking a demotion in order to get
off the road. It was tough going back into
the office and having to work with people
who said, "I told you so!"

If I had turned down the job, however, I
would have always wondered if I had
made the right decision. Now I know that
even one hour with my children is far
more important to me!

"I like to listen. I have learned a great deal from listening carefully. Most people never listen."

Ernest Hemingway

August

August 1

"We have two ears and only one tongue in order that we may hear more and speak less."
Diogenes Laertius

We have all been given *two ears* and *one mouth*. My mother used to say it is too bad that people do not use them in the proportion they were given to us!

In everyday communication, listening skills are actually used the most. In schools, communication skills are taught in the form of reading, writing, and speaking. Rarely is the focus on teaching listening skills.

Amazingly though, people who use sign language to communicate listen better than a person with no hearing loss. Why? Because they are focused on the hands of the other person, and they give the other person their *full* attention.

We all need to remember to stay focused and truly listen when someone is talking to us!

August 2

*"One of the best ways
to persuade others is
with your ears —
by listening to them."*
                    Dean Rusk

August 3

*"When the mind is thinking,
it is talking to itself."*
                    Plato

*Always question the "why";
don't be satisfied with only
knowing the "how".*

Don't just learn the *"how"* in your job,
also learn the *"why"*.

By understanding the "why", you are able
to constructively evaluate the job. Too
often, people only learn "how" to do the
job. When asked "why" they are doing a
job a certain way, their response is, "This is
the way we have always done it". But,
why, you ask, are you doing it this way?
They have no idea.

To know "how" to do something without
understanding the "why", is like being
illiterate. You can flip the pages of a book,
but the words won't have any meaning.

Don't just accept the "how". Question and
understand the "why"! By knowing the
"why", it's more than possible you may be
able to suggest improvements which, in
turn, can make your job more enjoyable
and more productive.

August 5

"There is a great difference
between knowing and
understanding: you can know
a lot about something and
not really understand it."

Charles F. Kettering

August 6

"The light of understanding has
shone upon my little pupil's mind,
and behold,
all things are changed."

Anne Sullivan

*"It's kind of fun
to do the impossible."*
Walt Disney

A lot of people thought Walt Disney's dream was ludicrous. Many people laughed at his ideas while others told him it was impossible.

Walt Disney had a dream, a strong determination, and a strong belief. He made it happen. If he had listened to all those who told him his dream was impossible, we would not have the Disney resorts we have today.

There are countless situations where individuals were told it was impossible, yet they went on to achieve success.

I believe it all comes down to your own outlook — if you think it is impossible, then it is. If you think it can be achieved, then what you see is not the impossible, but the end result.

August 8

*"Most of the things worth doing in
the world have been declared
impossible before they were done."*
Louis Brandeis

August 9

*"Attempt the impossible in
order to improve your work."*
Bette Davis

Constantly develop your communication skills as they are one of the key skills in life.

Communication skills are one of the most important skills we can develop.

Non verbal communication is as important as verbal and written communication skills. Watching a person's body language can help you become a better communicator. Look at these examples:

Uneasiness   not looking at the other person/ clearing throat

Frustration   short breaths/ running hand through hair

Co-operation   open hands/ tilted head/ sitting on edge of chair

Doubt   not looking at you/ arms crossed/ moving away

There are excellent books on body language in the public library including, "How to Read a Person Like a Book" by Gerard I. Nierenberg and Henry H. Calero.

AUGUST 11

*"The more elaborate our
means of communication,
the less we communicate."*
Joseph Priestley

AUGUST 12

*"It is not the language of painters,
but the language of nature which
one should listen to...
The feeling for things themselves,
for reality, is more important than
the feeling for pictures."*
Vincent Van Gogh

*How do you react to a
dead end road?
Do you say to yourself, I can't
go any farther, or, do you
back up and find another route to
reach your destination?*

As we travel down the road to success, at some point we will ultimately meet failure. What is important, however, is that we keep focused on our end goal. When failure occurs, a lot of people just see a dead end. It is only a dead end if you see it that way. All you have to do is back up and start at a different point.

How you see failure will ultimately determine whether you give up or try another way. Attitude plays a tremendously big role. How do you see your world? Do you have a determined attitude? Do you believe in yourself, or do you accept what others tell you about yourself? Are you quick to give up, or do you persevere? Scrutinize your attitude — how do you see your world?

Don't be blind and only see the dead end. Stop and determine what change in direction will get you back on track.

August 14

*"Men are born to succeed,
not fail."*
Henry David Thoreau

August 15

*"If I had permitted my failures,
or what seemed to me at the
time a lack of success,
to discourage me I cannot see any
way in which I would ever have
made progress."*
Calvin Coolidge

August 16

*"My interest is in the future
because I am going to spend
the rest of my life there."*
Charles F. Kettering

Focus on the future rather than dwelling on the past. Concentrate your thoughts on your dreams for the future.

We cannot change events in the past, nor can we rest on past accomplishments. Sometimes, people get so stuck in the past they can't see forward. They are actually moving backwards as life passes them by.

Think of your past as if you were driving down a one way street. Once you start down the street, you can't turn around and go in the other direction. It works the same way in life. If your choice is to spend your time and energy on what happened in the past, chances are you will not be able to turn around and move forward.

Remember, there is nothing you can do to change the events of the past, but there is a lot you can do about the future.

August 17

"*I like the dreams of the future
better than the history of the past.*"
Thomas Jefferson

August 18

"*When all else is lost,
the future still remains.*"
Christian Nestell Bovee

"As long as we have hope,
we have direction, the energy
to move,
and the map to move by.
We have a hundred alternatives,
a thousand paths and an infinity
of dreams.
Hopeful, we are halfway to where
we want to go;
hopeless, we are lost forever."
Hong Kong Proverb

Hope is one of the prime differences between successful people and those who can only see failure.

Successful people have hope because they can clearly see their goals.

People who only see failure have no hope because they see no light, they set no goals, and they see nothing accomplished.

Successful people see alternatives and are willing to try different ways. People who only see failure are unable to see another way and give up too easily.

August 20

*"In all things it is better
to hope than to despair."*
Goethe

August 21

*"There are no hopeless situations,
there are only men who have
grown helpless about them."*
Clare Boothe Luce

AUGUST 22

"All that we are is the result of
what we have thought.
The mind is everything.
What we think, we become."
                                    Buddha

As you were growing up, you may have been told over and over that you were good at doing something. You believed it.

Similarly, if you constantly tell people they are doing a good job, they will eventually believe it even if, in the beginning, they have doubts about their ability. In essence, we become what we believe.

If you find that you are doubting yourself, stop and reflect on all your past achievements. Be confident about yourself. Don't let other people erode your confidence. Successful people know that the greater their self-confidence, the greater their achievements.

Don't feed your mind with negative thoughts. If you do, you will come to believe them. The secret to self-confidence is to feed your mind with positive thoughts, and surround yourself with people who give you positive support!

AUGUST 23

*"As is our confidence,
so is our capacity."*
William Hazlitt

AUGUST 24

*"Nurture your mind
with great thoughts,
for you will never go any higher
than you think."*
Benjamin Disraeli

"When everything seems to be
going against you,
remember that the airplane takes
off against the wind, not with it."
Henry Ford

When everything is going along smoothly, you feel like nothing can stop you.

The true test of success comes when you run up against challenges, or people who put roadblocks in your path. How do you handle them?

Don't let setbacks get you down. Studying successful people will show you that they did not attain their success without first overcoming challenges.

When Beethoven was 26 years old, he started experiencing hearing problems which later became total deafness. Yet, Beethoven went on to compose some of his greatest works after his hearing loss. He had a strong passion for music, and even though everything seemed to be going against him, he showed tremendous determination to overcome his challenge and fulfil his desire to compose.

August 26

*"The true measure of a man is not
how he behaves in moments of
comfort and convenience
but how he stands at times of
controversy and challenges."*
Martin Luther King Jr.

August 27

*"Never bend your head.
Always hold it high.
Look the world straight in the eye."*
Helen Keller

August 28

*"Failures are made only by those
who fail to dare,
not by those who dare to fail."*
Lester B. Pearson

To assure that you will never experience failure:

- don't take a risk,
- don't attempt anything new,
- don't expand on your ideas,
- don't set goals.

Never to do any of these things actually guarantees you *will* fail.

In effect, to never experience a failure limits our learning and our growth.

Why?

We can learn from every failure. Failure is a golden opportunity to start again with more knowledge than we had before.

The most important element in the failure equation is your personal commitment to keep trying. Don't give up on your dreams because of one unsuccessful attempt!

AUGUST 29

*"The only time you don't fail is the
last time you try anything —
and it works."*

William Strong

AUGUST 30

*"It's hard to fail, but it is worse
never to have tried to succeed."*

James Thurber

August 31

*Is your attitude toward
your employer the same attitude
you'd demonstrate if you were
self-employed?*

For those of us who have chosen a corporate career rather than owning our own business, our attitude often needs readjustment.

Many corporate employees do not share the same attitude as those who own their own business. They expect the corporation to do things for them that they wouldn't ever dream of if they were self employed. We all need to undergo an attitude adjustment by realizing it is our responsibility to continue to improve our own skills, to contribute to the corporation's goals, and to share our ideas.

We need to adopt the perspective that we are the CEO of our own corporation — OURSELF!

We must demonstrate a continuous commitment to ensure our company (OURSELF) adds value!

"It is never too late to be what you might have been."

September

*"Nothing happens unless
first a dream."*
Carl Sandburg

It all began with a dream. James L. Gagan, founder of the United Consumers Club (UCC), was obsessed with a dream to provide a national buyer's club where members would enjoy huge savings by buying manufacturer's merchandise at cost.

Unrelenting in his passion to see his dream a reality, undisturbed by the many "nay sayers" including friends and relatives, he founded UCC in 1971, with only $1,000, and numerous business obstacles. There are over 500,000 UCC members in cities across the United States and Canada, all able to enjoy a better lifestyle because James Gagan had a dream.

What's your dream?

SEPTEMBER 2

"If you can dream it,
you can do it."

Walt Disney

SEPTEMBER 3

"Whatever you can do or dream
you can, begin it.
Boldness has genius, power,
and magic in it."

Goethe

SEPTEMBER 4

*"You can preach a better sermon
with your life than with your lips."*
Oliver Goldsmith

The personal example you set will do
more to convince someone than all the
eloquent speeches in the world. When you
expect others to demonstrate a certain type
of behaviour, ask yourself if your
behaviour exemplifies what you expect of
others.

If you take a piece of string and push it, it
will not go in the direction you want. But,
if you take that same piece of string and
pull it along, the string will move in the
same direction. That principle applies to
people. Don't push them along, pull them
along by your own actions, your
behaviour, your enthusiasm, and your
determination.

***What you do,
and how you act,
has more influence on people
than what you say!***

SEPTEMBER 5

"Example is not the main thing
in influencing others.
It is the only thing."
Albert Schweitzer

SEPTEMBER 6

"It is not fair to ask of others what
you are not willing to do yourself."
Eleanor Roosevelt

SEPTEMBER 7

"Obstacles are those frightful
things you see when you
take your eyes off the goal."
Hannah More

If we do not stay completely focused on our goal, any obstacle can stop us. Our focus must be glued to our long term goal like a stamp to a letter. By focusing on our long term goal, obstacles become nothing more than part of the process leading to success.

If you can create a vivid vision of what you want to achieve, and force yourself to concentrate on your goal, you will succeed. But, if you get stuck in seeing things just as they are, in seeing only the obstacles that are in your way, you drastically limit your chance of accomplishing your goal.

Successful people are determined, they have the ability to stick to it. They keep going. If one way doesn't work, they accept that and go on to try other ways until they succeed.

Concentrate on the end result.

September 8

*"Never look down to test
the ground before taking
your next step;
only he who keeps his eye
fixed on the far horizon will
find his right road."*
Dag Hammarskjold

September 9

*"Keep on going and the chances
are you will stumble on something,
perhaps when you are least
expecting it.
I have never heard of anyone
stumbling on something sitting
down."*
Charles F. Kettering

SEPTEMBER 10

*"The greatest mistake a man
can ever make is to be
afraid of making one."*
Elbert Hubbard

Making a mistake is one of life's greatest teachers.

Unfortunately, we have been taught to believe that making a mistake is wrong. Societal pressure pushes us to excel, to grow up thinking that making a mistake makes us less of a person. Yet, we can learn so much from a mistake. When the fear of making a mistake stops us from attempting new tasks or accepting new challenges, we're depriving ourselves of learning opportunities.

If we were successful at everything we did, if we never made a mistake, if we never had to change our perspective, we would learn very little.

We have to alter our attitude to accept mistakes as the master teacher. The lessons learned are the necessary ingredients of success.

September 11

*"We learn wisdom from failure
much more than from success;
we often discover what will do,
by finding out what will not do;
and probably he who never
made a mistake never made a
discovery."*

Samuel Smiles

September 12

*"A life spent in making mistakes
is not only more honourable
but more useful than a life
spent doing nothing."*

George Bernard Shaw

SEPTEMBER 13

*"What you don't see with
your eyes, don't invent
with your mouth."*
Jewish Proverb

G ossip is the greatest abuse of time and
energy. Everyone adds on their own
personal bias, interpretation, and
bitterness.

We used to play a children's game where
we all sat in a circle and one person would
whisper a sentence to the next person. By
the time it was repeated again to the first
person, the sentence was completely
different! Gossip is based on the same
principle.

People who spend their time finding fault
or gossiping about others, are certainly not
the kind of people you want as friends.

Those who gossip to you may also gossip
about you. If you can't say anything
positive about someone, don't say
anything.

Nothing productive is ever achieved as a
result of spreading, or listening to gossip.
Don't waste your time! You can make more
productive use of it.

SEPTEMBER 14

*"When you throw dirt,
you lose ground."*
                    Texan Proverb

SEPTEMBER 15

*"Two things are bad for the heart —
running up stairs and
running down people."*
                    Bernard Baruch

SEPTEMBER 16

*By not directly facing issues
that are bothering us, we are
creating internal road blocks.*

We cannot change what has happened,
but by facing it we can more easily
accept it.

All too often, we let little things upset us.
Most things in life are of little consequence
when you look at the big picture.

My great grandmother was widowed at a
very early age and left to raise four
children by herself during World War I.
She could have felt sorry for herself.
Instead, she got a job and held tight to the
conviction that she would raise her
children and give them all she could. Later
in her life, she had both her legs
amputated, but that didn't stop her either!
She lived to be 105 years old.

Here is a woman who had her share of
personal roadblocks, however, she faced
the issues and moved beyond them.

September 17

Keep all things in perspective!
What is of concern today, may be
of no consequence in the future.

September 18

"Men are disturbed, not by
the things that happen,
but by their opinion of the
things that happen."
Epictetus

SEPTEMBER 19

*Don't leave your destiny
up to someone else.*

What is your destiny in life?

Some people are not aware it's their choice to create their own destiny while others set personal goals and take responsibility for the direction of their lives.

You can surrender your destiny to the desires of others, or you can control your own destiny by establishing your goals and working steadily to attain them.

You have the choice.

What do you want? To control your own destiny, or let someone else control it?

September 20

*"Every man is the architect
of his own fortune."*

Appius Claudius

September 21

*"Destiny is not a matter of chance,
it is a matter of choice;
it is not a thing to be waited for,
it is a thing to be achieved."*

William Jennings Bryan

*"It's easy to have faith in
yourself and have discipline
when you're a winner,
when you're number one.
What you've got to have is faith
and discipline when you're
not yet a winner."*

Vince Lombardi

When things are not progressing as planned, when we are not as successful as we would like to be, when everything around us seems to be piling up, it is naturally the time to feel like quitting.

But take comfort in knowing that if there are no challenges to overcome, if everything worked as planned, we would not experience the richness of personal growth.

The secret in overcoming the desire to quit is to do what is unnatural by mustering the courage to stick with it. We must continually visualize how it will feel when we become number one. We must not succumb to the natural; we must do the unnatural by disciplining ourselves to keep going forward.

SEPTEMBER 23

*"Smooth seas do not
make skilful sailors."*
African Proverb

SEPTEMBER 24

*"It's not whether you get
knocked down.
It's whether you get up again."*
Vince Lombardi

SEPTEMBER 25

*"If the creator had a purpose
in equipping us with a neck,
he surely meant us to
stick it out."*

Arthur Koestler

We have to take a risk and move beyond our usual comfort zone if we want to be successful. In other words, if we want to have more than we currently have, we need to *"stick our neck out"*.

There is no absolute security in life. We need to take a chance if we want to see change.

Look carefully at successful people. They did not attain positions of power, or amass wealth, or create masterpieces by sitting back and doing what they always did. They had to take a risk, and stick their neck out. Stick your neck out!

Opportunities are not handed out on a silver platter, you must go after them!

SEPTEMBER 26

*"Great deeds are usually
wrought at great risk."*
                    Herodotus

SEPTEMBER 27

*"Only those who dare to fail
greatly can ever achieve greatly."*
                    Robert F. Kennedy

*"People would rather be shown
how valuable you are, not told."*
                          Roger W. Babson

Let me tell you a story of two people I
worked with ten years ago. Both of
these individuals were the same age, and
approximate intelligence. Both wanted to
progress in their careers. But, there was
one major difference between them. One
just talked and complained about not
getting ahead while the other person took
the initiative by taking courses, and
finding solutions to obstacles.

Now, 10 years later, the person who talked
and complained is still talking and
complaining and still remains in the same
position. The person who took the
initiative and found solutions has been
promoted several times.

What you have accomplished in the past is
a much stronger example than talking
about what you are capable of doing in the
future!

Actions do speak louder than words!

SEPTEMBER 29

*"You can't build a reputation
on what you are going to do."*
Henry Ford

SEPTEMBER 30

*"We judge ourselves by what
we feel capable of doing,
while others judge us by
what we have already done."*
Henry Wadsworth Longfellow

October

OCTOBER 1

*"Ask not what your country
can do for you, ask what
you can do for your country."*
John F. Kennedy

The above philosophy can be used in all areas of your life.

In your personal life, rather than expecting people to do something for you, ask yourself what can you do for them.

In your professional life, rather than expecting your employer to do something for you, ask yourself what you can do for your employer.

You will double your success in all areas of life by asking yourself what you can do for others.

I truly believe that when you do something good, it comes back to you in many positive ways!

October 2

*"He stands erect by
bending over the fallen.
He rises by lifting others."*
    Robert G. Ingersoll

October 3

*"What goes around,
comes around!"*
    Author Unknown

OCTOBER 4

*"The only way to have a
friend is to be one."*
Ralph Waldo Emerson

Friendship is not like a product to be used when you need it.

To be a friend means that you are willing to give of yourself not only through the good times, but also during the bad times.

To be a friend means encouraging strengths in others and accepting their weaknesses; in other words, accepting them for who they are.

In the end, to be a friend means giving freely and not expecting anything in return.

What is your definition of a friend?

*Do you live up to your own definition
with your friends?*

October 5

*"Friendship without self-interest
is one of the rare and beautiful
things of life."*

James F. Byrnes

October 6

*"When a person is down in the
world, an ounce of help is better
than a pound of preaching."*

Edward G. Bulwer-Lytton

*"Goals help you overcome
short-term problems."*

Hannah More

To have a goal is like having a road map. It shows you where to go, and where not to go. Would you begin a trip to an unknown city without first looking at a map? Probably not.

Amazingly though, many people conduct their lives without any personal road map to success. Goals are like a map. They help us determine where we want to end up, and give us personal direction on which to focus our energy.

Once you decide what it is you want, set your sights and start taking action to achieve it. This "action" is the commitment on your part. And, once you are committed to a goal, really committed, problems are short term. With your entire focus on your goal, you will reach levels of achievement that you never thought possible.

**Without goals, you will end up going nowhere, or,
you will end up following someone else's map!**

October 8

*"The world makes way for the man
who knows where he is going."*
Ralph Waldo Emerson

October 9

*"If one advances confidently
in the direction of his dreams,
and endeavours to live the life
which he has imagined, he will
meet with a success unexpected
in common hours."*
Henry David Thoreau

Over the course of 41 years:
His sister died.
He failed in business.
His sweetheart died.
He was defeated for Congress
twice.
His son, Eddie, died.
He was defeated for Senate twice.
He was defeated for
Vice-President.
But on the 42nd year, he was
elected President of
the United States!
The man:
Abraham Lincoln.

If you ever needed just one example of a person who had perseverance and determination, it was Abraham Lincoln.

Perseverance allows us to continue our quest and focus our energy on reaching our goal no matter what the odds. It bolsters our strength to face an obstacle or difficulty.

Do you possess the same kind of perseverance and determination as Lincoln?

October 11

"It's not that I'm so smart, it's just that I stay with problems longer."
Albert Einstein

October 12

Using patience and perseverance to tackle obstacles will ensure we overcome any obstacle.

OCTOBER 13

*"One machine can do the work
of fifty ordinary men. No
machine can do the work of
one extraordinary man."*
Elbert Hubbard

Are you an ordinary person?

Do you do only what you have to at work
and not a speck more? Be that one
extraordinary person. Adopt the attitude of
doing more than what is expected.

You can be the most brilliant person in the
world, but this does not, in itself,
guarantee success. To achieve success, you
must be willing to put out significant
effort.

As technology continues to advance, jobs
will continue to change. Companies keep
the extraordinary staff over the ordinary
staff. Don't allow your skills and talents to
be ordinary. Continue to improve your
skills, add new skills, and become the
extraordinary person!

OCTOBER 14

*"Opportunity is missed by most
people because it is dressed in
overalls and looks like work."*
Thomas A. Edison

OCTOBER 15

*"Genius is one percent inspiration
and
ninety-nine percent perspiration."*
Thomas A. Edison

OCTOBER 16

"You may delay, but time will not."
Benjamin Franklin

By delaying, you are procrastinating.

Procrastination not only steals your time, it steals your money, your happiness, your life. If you continually neglect what needs to be done today, it soon becomes a habit. After a period of time, a habit is very difficult to change. Procrastination can destroy careers, businesses and relationships.

Here are some ways to avoid procrastination:
- Prioritize; determine what is most important. Focus your attention on the highest priorities.
- Set a deadline for yourself.
- Break projects into a series of smaller tasks; this will help reduce the feeling of being overwhelmed.
- Reward yourself once you have completed a task or a project.
- Most importantly, take that first step! The first step is almost always the most difficult!

We can never regain time once it is gone!

OCTOBER 17

*"Procrastination is the
thief of time."*
Edward Young

OCTOBER 18

*"The art of being wise is the art
of knowing what to overlook."*
William James

OCTOBER 19

*"You must not allow yourself
to dwell for a single moment
on any kind of negative thought."*
Emmet Fox

When life seems overwhelming, are you able to look ahead and see light at the end of the tunnel?

Sometimes, life's challenges are tough to deal with. You will succeed if you focus your thoughts on how to overcome the challenge.

Negative thoughts are like weeds in a garden.

Once a weed is allowed to flourish, the garden is quickly overtaken. But, if you weed the garden before the weeds spread, you will end up with a beautiful and bountiful garden.

You are the only one who can control the way you think. Make sure you nourish the positive thoughts, and weed out the negative ones!

OCTOBER 20

"The only difference between a rut and a grave is their dimensions."
Ellen Glasgow

OCTOBER 21

"We are all in the gutter, but some of us are looking at the stars."
Oscar Wilde

OCTOBER 22

"Never bear more than
one trouble at a time.
Some people bear three kinds —
all they have had,
all they have now,
and all they expect to have."
Edward Everett Hale

Think of your past troubles as lessons to help you with the challenges you face now.

Eliminate today's troubles by finding solutions, and then concentrate your energy on implementing those solutions.

As for the troubles of tomorrow, either completely forget them, or take whatever action is necessary to avoid them or minimize them.

Remember the song,

"Don't worry, be happy"?
It is good advice!

October 23

*"Worry gives a small thing
a big shadow."*
Swedish Proverb

October 24

*"Worry is interest paid on
trouble before it is due."*
William R. Inge

OCTOBER 25

"Habit is a cable;
we weave a thread of it every day,
and at last we cannot break it."
Horace Mann

What habits are you weaving every day? What are you weaving that will be difficult to break? Look closely at your daily activities for part of the answer.

Do your habits support what you want to become, or do they form unnecessary road blocks that prevent you from becoming what you want.

We can all choose the habits we want. They can be very productive, or they can be unproductive.

For example, what about the person who comes home every day and sits and watches TV until bedtime. Will watching TV develop habits that moves them closer to their goals?

Are you weaving good habits?

OCTOBER 26

"Sow an act and
you reap a habit.
Sow a habit and
you reap a character.
Sow a character
and you reap a destiny."
                            Charles Reade

OCTOBER 27

"Ninety-nine percent of failures
come from people who have the
habit of making excuses."
                            George W. Carver

OCTOBER 28

*"People ask you for criticism,
but they only want praise."*
W. Somerset Maugham

Before you give criticism, always give praise. Many of us have a habit of seeing and focusing only on the negative.

To motivate both children and adults to change and improve, they first need to hear what they have done well.

Criticizing without providing positive comments does not motivate people. We all need to receive praise and encouragement.

Although mistakes must be pointed out so learning can take place, the absence of encouragement or praise diminishes a person's confidence or self-esteem.

One of the secrets to success in working with and developing people is to give them honest praise, constant encouragement and constructive criticism, in that order.

October 29

"Correction does much, but encouragement does more."

Goethe

October 30

"He who praises everybody, praises nobody."

Samuel Johnson

Risk

"To laugh is to risk *appearing the fool. To weep is to* risk *appearing sentimental. To reach out for another is to* risk *involvement. To express feelings is to* risk *exposing your true self. To place your ideas, your dreams, before the crowd is to* risk *their loss. To love is to* risk *not being loved in return. To live is to* risk *dying. To hope is to* risk *despair. To try is to* risk *failure. But,* risk *must be taken, because the greatest hazard in life is to* risk *nothing. The person who* risks *nothing...has nothing...is nothing...does nothing. They may avoid suffering, and sorrow but simply cannot learn, feel, change, grow, love or live. Chained by attitudes, we become slaves, we forfeit our freedom.*

Only the person who takes risks is free!"   Author Unknown

The above says it all!

"We all live in suspense from day to day; in other words, you are the hero of your own story."
Mary McCarthy

November

*"Only a mediocre person
is always at his best."*
W. Somerset Maugham

Mediocre people do only what they have to do to get by and not an ounce more.

- They never take the initiative to learn new things.
- They never take action that would put them at the risk of failing.
- They never set goals that require them to stretch, or work harder, or smarter.
- They believe they are at their best, so there is no reason to do any more.

This type of person will never achieve more, or be more. They will be in the same position five years from now as they are today.

I have worked with a few mediocre people over the years. They have always complained they were not progressing, yet they did absolutely nothing to help themselves.

213

November 2

*"People who are unable to motivate
themselves must be content with
mediocrity, no matter how
impressive their other talents."*
Andrew Carnegie

November 3

*"If one is too lazy to think,
too vain to do a thing badly,
too cowardly to admit it,
no one will never attain wisdom."*
Cyril Connolly

"Common sense is instinct,
and enough of it is genius."
Josh Billings

I have been in situations where someone who is more educated, or who is in a more senior position, made a decision I disagreed with. My common sense told me that it was the wrong decision. But, I thought they must know what they were doing because they were more educated, and in a more senior position. As it turned out, this was not always the case!

Far too many of us blindly accept a decision of a superior without challenging the assumptions upon which the decision is based.

On the other hand, showing the confidence to challenge decisions based on our own common sense can lead to more thoughtful decisions.

November 5

"*Common sense is
genius in homespun.*"
Alfred North Whitehead

November 6

"*Common sense is the knack
of seeing things as they are,
and doing things as they
ought to be done.*"
Josh Billings

*"Flaming enthusiasm, backed
by horse sense and persistence,
is the quality that most frequently
makes for success."*
Dale Carnegie

Having enthusiasm in performing any task gives you an abundance of energy. Showing enthusiasm also motivates others around you.

An acronym for enthusiasm:
Energy
Nimble
Tenacious
Happy
Unbeatable
Self-confident
Inexhaustible
Achievable
Success
Motivated

Put lots of enthusiasm in all you do!

November 8

"Every production of genius must be the production of enthusiasm."
Benjamin Disraeli

November 9

"You can do anything if you have enthusiasm. Enthusiasm is the yeast that makes your hopes rise to the stars. With it, there is accomplishment. Without it there are only alibis."
Henry Ford

"The most thoroughly wasted
of all days is that on which
one has not laughed."
Nicolas Chamfort

A re you guilty of taking life too
seriously?

One of the keys to happiness is the ability
to not only laugh at life, but to be able to
laugh at yourself.

Laughter releases tension and eases stress.
There is an old saying that laughter is the
best medicine — how true! You always feel
better when you laugh.

Just think of how you feel when you hear
someone else laughing. Some people have
such an infectious laugh that they actually
make you smile in spite of yourself.

Let your laughter infect
those around you!

November 11

*"Laughter is the tonic, the relief,
the surcease for pain."*
Charlie Chaplin

November 12

*"Laugh, and the world
laughs with you;
Weep, and you weep alone."*
Ella W. Wilcox

*"There are many ways of
going forward, but only
one way of standing still."*
Franklin D. Roosevelt

Sometimes, due to unforeseen challenges, we get discouraged and don't reach our goals. As hard as it may be, we must always take continual action to keep going forward. We may even have to take a different route, or explore different ways of reaching our goal.

But, one thing is for sure, if we do nothing, we get nothing.

We often put things off because we think we do not have enough time. But doing just a little bit during the time you have puts you further ahead than if you did nothing at all. To consistently make progress you must be willing to steadily apply yourself to required tasks.

Three of the most important ways to consistently apply yourself are to: break your goal or project into small action steps; schedule time to complete each step; and third, don't procrastinate — just do it!

NOVEMBER 14

*"No matter how far you have gone
on a wrong road, turn back."*
Turkish Proverb

NOVEMBER 15

*"Don't be afraid of growing slowly,
be afraid only of standing still."*
Chinese Proverb

NOVEMBER 16

*"Whether you think you can or
think you can't — you are right."*
Henry Ford

Our thoughts do in fact shape our whole life, and our daily happiness. We have all heard the saying, "you are what you eat". Well, the same is true of your thoughts, "you are what you think".

If you think *"you can"*, then anything is possible. But, if you think *"you can't"*, then you are defeated before you even begin!

Your mind is tremendously powerful. Your own thoughts determine your success. Once you start to think, "I can't," your subconscious mind will work to turn this thought into a reality.

Some people search their entire lifetime trying to find happiness and success. They never discover that the secret is all in how they think and how they view life.

Have an "I Can" attitude towards life!

NOVEMBER 17

*"Our life is what our
thoughts make it."*
Marcus Aurelius

NOVEMBER 18

*"They are able because
they think they are able."*
Virgil

*"I'm a great believer in luck,
and I find the harder I work,
the more I have of it."*
Thomas Jefferson

L uck comes to those who work. You may think that other people are just plain lucky. The truth is, you do not see the effort they put in. Like everything else in this life, you must put in the effort.

Good fortune does not happen because of luck. When someone gets a promotion, some people see this as luck. If they took a closer look, however, they would soon recognize how much harder successful people have worked, how much effort they've given, and how much dedication and commitment they've demonstrated in order to go that extra mile.

If those who believe in luck saw all of the required effort, then they would truly understand what luck really is!

NOVEMBER 20

"It will generally be found that men who are constantly lamenting their ill luck are only reaping the consequences of their own neglect, mismanagement, and improvidence, or want of application."

Samuel Smiles

NOVEMBER 21

"I don't know anything about luck. I've never banked on it, and I'm afraid of people who do. Luck to me is something else; hard work and realizing what is - opportunity and what isn't."

Lucille Ball

*Don't put off capturing
your dreams. When you grow
older, you will deeply regret not
turning your dreams into reality!*

Don't be one of those people who think,
"I wonder what would have
happened if I'd..."

When you allow dust to gather on your
goal because you believe it is too difficult,
or you say you are too busy, the day will
come when you'll say: "It might have
been".

Write out your goals on paper, and commit
to do them. Start taking action immediately
towards accomplishing them.

Before you start to work on your goals,
decide right now that excuses are simply
challenges to test your will to overcome
and succeed.

There can be nothing worse than growing
old and realizing your life is not what you
wanted.

*You are never too old to set new goals
and start taking action!*

November 23

*"Don't go around saying the
world owes you a living.
The world owes you nothing.
It was here first."*

Mark Twain

November 24

*"Of all the sad words of tongue
or pen, the saddest are these:
'It might have been'."*

John Greenlead Whittier

November 25

*"We are prone to judge success
by the index of our salaries or
the size of our automobile rather
than by the quality of our service
and relationship to humanity."*
Martin Luther King Jr.

What is success?

To some it is money; to others it is position;
yet to others, it is power.

In developing your own definition of
success, think of others and how you can
help them. If success means money to you,
then donate money to a worthwhile
charity. If success means a position of
status, then share your knowledge with
others. If success means power to you, then
use that to advance worthwhile causes.

All to often, we get caught up in all the
things we want, and forget to give back to
the world.

Our society seems to place more value on
how much we have rather than how much
we give. What a different world it would
be if society placed more value on how
much we gave!

November 26

*"We make a living by what we get.
We make a life by what we give."*
Winston Churchill

November 27

*"Every good act is charity.
A man's true wealth hereafter is
the good that he does in
this world to his fellows."*
Mohammed

*Perseverance allows you
to get back on track when
you hit a detour!*

Perseverance is the ability to keep going in the face of continuous challenges. It is the ability to disregard distractions and to stay focused.

You may have to take detours to get to your end goal. But, as long as you persevere and realize that the detour is simply another alternative path in the direction of your goal, you will continue to move forward.

Those who see a detour as a reason to quit, lack perseverance. You will always face challenges as you work towards your goals. Your ability to persevere will determine your ultimate success!

It takes effort and belief to persevere and stay dedicated to accomplish your goal. When you find yourself doubting whether the effort is worth it, visualize how you will feel and what you will have once your goal is completed. Persevere, and don't let any self-doubt distract you.

November 29

"Results!
Why man, I have gotten
a lot of results.
I know of several thousand things
that won't work."
Thomas A. Edison

November 30

"Great works are performed not
by strength but by perseverance."
Samuel Johnson

December

"Don't be afraid to stumble.
Any inventor will tell you
that you don't follow a plan
far before you strike a snag.
If, out of 100 ideas you get
***one** that works, it's enough."*
Charles F. Kettering

In studying successful people, you will find that many of them had an abundance of ideas that did not work. Yet, they kept going and didn't get discouraged by unsuccessful attempts. After many attempts, in some cases, they found *one* idea that did work, and that *one* idea led them to their ultimate success.

Finding that *one* idea requires an intense desire. Intense desire also empowers you to discover hidden talents.

Successful people are not afraid to confront failure when their first idea fails. They do not quit because they know to do so would forever rob them of discovering that one idea that could work.

DECEMBER 2

*"It sometimes seems that intense
desire creates not only its own
opportunities, but its own talents."*
Eric Hoffer

DECEMBER 3

*"When we are flat on our backs
there is no way to look but up."*
Roger W. Babson

December 4

*"The future belongs to
those who believe in the
beauty of their dreams."*
Eleanor Roosevelt

Your dreams are the gateway to your future. You must be able to visualize your dream as if it is already completed. This takes clarity and passion.

Many athletes use visualization skills to help them achieve their dream of winning. They visualize themselves winning a gold medal long before they ever compete. They visualize themselves successfully performing every necessary action that will lead them to victory.

Visualization is especially helpful when you feel discouraged because it will help keep you on track to reach your goal.

Use the power of visualization as your rehearsal for reaching each and every goal that you set.

December 5

"There is no use whatever
trying to help people who
do not help themselves.
You cannot push anyone up
a ladder unless he be
willing to climb himself."
Andrew Carnegie

December 6

"The most pathetic person
in the world is someone
who has sight but has no vision."
Helen Keller

December 7

*"We do not care of what we have,
but we cry when it is lost."*
Russian Proverb

Have you ever moved to a new city, or left one job for another?

Too often, we don't appreciate or recognize the value of the things we have, until they are gone.

Once gone, we miss the everyday things that we casually take for granted.

The saddest experience we can have is when someone close to us dies. Then, it is too late to express our appreciation to them for the joy and friendship they brought into our lives.

We need to take time to truly appreciate the things we have now before they are gone forever.

Many times we wish for better things when we should fully appreciate the bounty we already possess.

December 8

*"The more one does and sees and
feels, the more one is able to do,
and the more genuine may be
one's appreciation of fundamental
things like home, and love, and
understanding companionship."*

Amelia Earhart

December 9

*"Happiness always looks small
while you hold it in your hands,
but let it go, and you learn at
once how big and precious it is."*

Maxim Gorky

"When I was a young man, I wanted to change the world.

I found it was difficult to change the world, so I tried to change my nation. When I found I couldn't change the nation, I began to focus on my town. I couldn't change the town and as an older man, I tried to change my family. Now, as an old man, I realize the only thing I can change is myself, and suddenly I realize that if long ago I had changed myself, I could have made an impact on my family. My family and I could have made an impact on our town. Their impact could have changed the nation and I could indeed have changed the world."

Unknown Monk 1100 A.D.

G reat words for reflection if we rashly attempt to change something or someone else other than ourselves!

December 11

*"I wanted to change the world.
But I have found that the only
thing one can be sure of
changing is oneself."*
Aldous Huxley

December 12

*"Change your thoughts,
and you change your world."*
Norman Vincent Peale

*"Time is the coin of your life.
It is the only coin you have, and
you can determine how it will be
spent. Be careful lest you let other
people spend it for you."*
Carl Sandburg

We never seem to have enough time!

Quite frankly, I don't think "time" is the problem. The real problem is the number of activities or tasks that we take on. A sign of our time is that we forget how to say "no", and take on far too many things.

Our time is like jam, the more you try to spread it, the thinner it gets. We need to be realistic about the amount of time we have available.

We need to maintain a proper balance in our life by allocating the time we have. There are occasions where saying no is the best time management practice there is. We need to determine what activities best utilize our time in order to achieve the results we desire in all areas of our life!

DECEMBER 14

"Beware of little expenses.
A small leak will sink
a great ship."
Benjamin Franklin

DECEMBER 15

"Time is like money,
the less we have of it to spare
the further we make it go."
Josh Billings

"Learning you get from school.
Education you get from life."
Mark Twain

Undoubtedly, education is becoming more and more important in today's society.

True wisdom and knowledge only comes when you apply your knowledge to real life situations.

Only through real time application are you actually able to test theory against reality, and gain valuable experiences.

How we choose to utilize our real life education will dramatically determine our success. This will not only determine our professional success, but our personal happiness as well.

Look at education as a
continuous life long journey.

DECEMBER 17

*"Ask the experienced rather
than the learned."*

Arabic Proverb

DECEMBER 18

*"When I was a boy of fourteen,
my father was so ignorant
I could hardly stand to have
the old man around.
But when I got to be twenty-one,
I was astonished at how much
the old man had learned in
seven years."*

Mark Twain

DECEMBER 19

*"The time to repair the roof
is when the sun is shining."*
John F. Kennedy

What motivates you to change, to take action?

Those who wait to take action until they find themselves in a desperate situation face more difficulties than they need to.

One of the saddest examples is an employed person who has the opportunity to take courses to improve his skills, but instead, does nothing until he finds he no longer has a job.

Keep improving your skills, and education, and you will greatly improve your odds of success.

**Don't wait for
desperate times!**

DECEMBER 20

*Make choices today that
allows you to enjoy not
only today, but tomorrow.*

DECEMBER 21

*"They who know how to employ
opportunities will often find that
they can create them; and what we
can achieve depends less on the
amount of time we possess than
on the use we make of our time."*
                                    John S. Mill

DECEMBER 22

*"Few men are lacking capacity,
but they fail because they are
lacking in application."*
Calvin Coolidge

The "I can't" attitude stops us all, and the following story clearly demonstrates this truism:

A friend of mine was told by his high school principal that he would never amount to anything — he didn't have what it took to be successful. After graduating from high school with barely passing grades, he went from one mediocre job to another with his principal's words ringing loud in his thoughts.

After reading several success stories of great men who had also been told they would never accomplish anything, he realized he was living a life imposed by someone else's view — certainly not his own. Armed with a new vision he created for his life, he successfully wrote a university entrance exam, and went on to complete his graduate studies.

DECEMBER 23

*"Mediocrity obtains more
with application than
superiority without it."*
Balthasar Gracian

DECEMBER 24

*"I'm looking for a lot of men who
have an infinite capacity to not
know what can't be done."*
Henry Ford

December 25

"There is more happiness in giving than in receiving."

Acts, 20:35

For most of us, Christmas is a wonderful time of year!

Imagine what Christmas is like for families with children where there is not enough money for groceries, let alone presents.

At some point in our lives, misfortune may visit our homes. For those who experience misfortune at Christmas, it is even more difficult.

Especially at this time of year, we should share our good fortune with those who are less fortunate.

Have a wonderful Christmas!

DECEMBER 26

"Whenever you are to do a thing,
though it can never be known
but to yourself,
ask yourself how you would act
were all the world looking at you
and act accordingly."
Thomas Jefferson

DECEMBER 27

"One kernel is felt in a hogshead;
one drop of water helps to swell
the ocean; a spark of fire helps to
give light to the world.
None are too small, too feeble, too
poor to be of service.
Think of this and act."
Hannah More

December 28

*"A smile goes a long way, but
you must start it on its journey."*
Helen Keller

Have you ever driven slowly through a small community and someone walking along smiles and nods to you?

Or have you ever walked by a stranger who smiles and says "Hi there"?

Unfortunately, this show of friendliness seems to happen more in smaller communities than it does in larger cities. It seems that in the larger cities everyone is too busy to smile, or no one trusts anyone else. We need to smile more — it will turn the concrete of the city into sunshine.

*Do you wait until someone smiles and
acknowledges you,
or,
are you the one who starts the smile on its
journey?*

DECEMBER 29

"Remember that happiness
is as contagious as gloom.
It should be the first duty of
those who are happy to let
others know of their gladness."
Maurice Maeterlinck

DECEMBER 30

"Life is made up,
not of great sacrifices or duties,
but of little things,
in which smiles and kindness,
and small obligations win and
preserve the heart."
Humphrey Davy

DECEMBER 31

"Never, never, never quit!"
Winston Churchill

By setting clear and realistic goals, by never giving up, and by working hard to achieve them, you will accomplish more in your life time than most.

With each new year comes new ambitions, new knowledge, and new goals.

Record the goals that you achieve each year. In a few years, you will have a long list of accomplishments. Feel proud, YOU DID IT.

If you get discouraged, or start doubting yourself, go back to your list of achievements and remember how much you have already accomplished.

Never, never, abandon yourself! Within you lies the potential for unlimited growth!

May the coming year bring you happiness and success!

253

References

Recommended Books

ANDERSON, NANCY. *Work with Passion, How to do what you love for a living.* San Rafael, California: New World Library, 1995.

ASH, MARY KAY. *Mary Kay, The Success Story of America's Most Dynamic Businesswoman.* New York: Harper & Row, Publishers, 1981.

ANTHONY, DR. ROBERT. *The Ultimate Secrets of Total Self-Confidence.* New York: The Berkley Publishing Group, 1979.

BACH, RICHARD. *Illusions, The Adventures of a Reluctant Messiah.* New York: Bantam Doubleday Dell Publishing Group, Inc., 1977.

BRANS, JO. *Take Two, True stories of real people who dared to change their lives.* New York: Doubleday, a division of Bantam Doubleday Dell Publishing Group, Inc., 1989.

BRISTOL, CLAUDE M. *The Magic of Believing.* New York: Cornerstone Library, 1967.

BROWN JR., H. JACKSON. *Life's Little Instruction Book.* Nashville, Tennessee: Rutledge Hill Press, 1993

BURKA, JANE B., and YUEN, LENORA M. *Procrastination: why you do it, what to do about it.* Reading, Massachusetts: Addison-Wesley Publishing Company, 1983.

CARNEGIE, DALE. *How to Win Friends and Influence People.* New York: Simon & Schuster, 1936. New York: Pocket Books, 1981.

CIMMER, HENRY B. *The Wealthy Procrastinator, A story of financial planning for those who thought it was too late!* Calgary, Alberta: Springbank Publishing, 1993.

CLASON, GEORGE S. *The Richest Man in Babylon, The success secrets of the ancients-the most inspiring book on wealth ever written!* New York: Penguin Books USA Inc., 1955.

COVEY, STEPHEN R. *The 7 Habits of Highly Effective People, Powerful Lessons in Personal Change.* New York: Fireside, 1989.

DYER, DR. WAYNE. *Pulling Your Own Strings, dynamic techniques for dealing with other people and mastering your own life.* New York: The Hearst Corporation, 1978.

_____.*The Sky's the Limit.* New York: Simon & Schuster, Inc., 1980.

FRIEDMAN, MARTHA. *The Fear of Success, Why and how we defeat ourselves and what to do about it.* New York: Warner Books, Inc., 1980.

FISHER, MARK. *The Millionaire's Secrets, Life Lessons in Wisdom and Wealth.* New York: Simon & Schuster, 1996.

GAGAN, JAMES L., with SHOOK, ROBERT L. *America's Best Kept Secret.* Chicago, Illinois: Contemporary Books, Inc., 1991.

GAWAIN, SHAKTI. *Creative Visualization, use the power of your imagination to create what you want in your life.* San Rafael, California 1978: New World Library, 1991.

GIVENS, CHARLES J. *Super Self, Doubling Your Personal Effectiveness.* New York: Simon & Schuster, 1993.

HANSON, PETER G., M.D. *The Joy of Stress.* Islington, Ontario: Hanson Stress Management Organization, 1986.

HELMSTETTER, SHAD. *What to Say When You Talk to Your Self, the major new breakthrough to Managing People, Yourself, and Success.* Scottsdae, Arizona: Grindle Press, 1986.

_____.*You Can Excel in Times of Change.* New York: Simon & Schuster Inc., 1991.

HILL, NAPOLEON. *Think and Grow Rich.* New York: Ballantine Books 1983.

References

HILL, NAPOLEON. *Napoleon Hill's A Year of Growing Rich, 52 Steps to Achieving Life's Rewards.* New York: Penguin Books USA Inc., 1993.

HOPKINS, TOM. *The Official Guide To Success.* Scottsdale, Arizona: Tom Hopkins International Ltd, 1982.

HYATT, CAROLE. *Lifetime employability, How to become indispensable.* New York: Mastermedia Limited, 1995.

JENSEN, PETER K. *The Inside Edge: high performance through mental fitness.* Toronto, Ontario: Macmillan Canada, 1992.

KASSORLA, DR. IRENE C. *Go For It! How to win at Love, Work and Play.* New York: Dell Publishing Co., Inc., 1984.

MANDINO, OG. *A Better Way to Live.* New York: Bantam Doubleday Dell Publishing Group, Inc., 1990.

McGINNIS, ALAN LOY. *Bringing out the Best in People, how to enjoy helping others excel.* Minneapolis, Minnesota: Augsburg Publishing House, 1985.

_____. *The Power of Optimism, mastering the 12 characteristics of tough-minded optimists to bring out the best in yourself, take charge of your life, keep enthusiasm high.* New York: Harper & Row, Publishers, Inc., 1990.

MORTELL, ART. *The Courage to Fail.* New York: McGraw-Hill, Inc., 1973.

MURPHY, DR. JOSEPH. *The Power of Your Subconscious Mind.* Englewood Cliffs, New Jersey: Prentice-Hall, Inc., 1963.

NIERENBERG, GERARD I. and CALERO, HENRY H. *How to Read a Person Like a Book, the classic guide to interpreting body language.* New York: Simon & Schuster, Inc., 1986.

O'GRADY, DENNIS. *Taking the fear out of changing.* Holbrook, Massachusetts: Bob Adams, Inc., 1994.

PEALE, NORMAN VINCENT. *The Power of Positive Thinking.* Englewood Cliffs, New Jersey: Prentice-Hall, 1954. New York: Fawcett, 1978.

References

POPCORN, FAITH. *Clicking: 16 trends to future fit your life, your work, and your business.* New York: HarperCollins, 1996.

WAITLEY, DENIS. *The Double Win, success is a 2-way street.* Old Tappan, New Jersey: Fleming H. Revell Company, 1985.

____. *The Seeds of Greatness, The ten best-kept secrets of total success.* New York: Simon & Schuster, Inc., 1983.

____. *Timing is Everything, Turning Your Seasons of Success into Maximum Opportunities.* Nashville,Tennessee: Thomas Nelson, Inc. Publishers, 1992.

WILLIAMS, A. L. *All You Can Do is All You Can Do but all you can do is enough.* New York: Random House, Inc., 1988.

RASKIN, PATRICIA J. *Success, Your Dream and You.* Malibu, California: Roundtable Publishing Inc., 1991.

ROBERT, GERRY. *Conquering Life's Obstacles.* Agincourt, Ontario: Beaumont International, 1990.

SABINE, GORDON and PATRICIA. *Books That Made the Difference, what people told us.* Hamden, Connecticut: Library Professional Publication, 1983.

SCHWARTZ, DAVID J., PH. D. *The Magic of Thinking Big, Acquire the secrets of success...achieve everything you've always wanted: personal property, financial security, power and influence, the ideal job, satisfying relationships, a rewarding and enjoyable life.* New York: Simon & Schuster, Inc., 1987.

SCHULLER, ROBERT. *The Be (Happy) Attitudes, eight positive attitudes that can transform your life!* Waco, Texas: Word Books Publisher, 1985.

TEMPLETON, CHARLES. *Succeeding.* Toronto, Ontario: Stoddart Publishing Co. Limited, 1989.

WALTHER GEORGE R. *Power Talking, 50 ways to say what you mean and get what you want.* New York: The Berkley Publishing Group, 1991.

Index by Subject

Index by Author

265

Quotes by Catherine Pulsifer —

Order Form

Title	Cost Per Item	Quantity	Total
Wings for Goals	$11.00 CDN $7.95 US		
Wings for Work	$11.00 CDN $7.95 US		
Wings of Wisdom	$23.95 CDN $16.95 US		

Sub total _____

Add $3.00 Shipping & Handling for first book,
plus $2.00 for each additional book. _____

Cdn residents (excluding NB, NS, NF) add 7% GST _____

NB, NS, NF residents add 15% HST _____
(GST #87798 6455)

TOTAL ENCLOSED _____

Name: (Please print) _____

Address: _____

City: _____ Prov/State: _____ Country: _____

Postal/Zip: _____ Telephone: _____ (For order verification)

Register your e-mail address for new product information:
_____

Make check/money order (sorry, no COD orders) **payable to:**
Anncath-Roby Books
Mail to:

Anncath-Roby Books
P.O. Box 21085
Mississauga ON Canada L5N 6A2

**Guarantee: I understand that I may return any book for a full refund
for any reason up to 90 days after purchase, no questions asked.**

Other books by Catherine Pulsifer available through
authorized dealers or Anncath-Roby Books:

- **Wings for Goals: How To Use Three Easy Steps To
  Change Your Life Forever!**

*Learn how to get what you want, desire, or need in your life by
using the 3 easy and fully explained steps — YOU Deserve it!
Have more, be more — do what you've always wanted to do in
YOUR life. Start right now.*
*ISBN 0-9683013-1-2. Softcover, 58 pg. Includes references and index.
$11.00 CDN, $7.95 U.S.*

- **Wings for Work: Learn How To Develop and Use The
  Three Key Qualities That Successful People Have
  Mastered!**

*Have you ever wondered why other people get ahead at work,
or why they receive greater pay increases or larger bonuses?
Stop wondering and join them. Don't just find out why — learn
how to develop and use these same key qualities that can make
YOU outstanding!*
*ISBN 0-9683013-2-0. Softcover, 58 pg. Includes index.
$11.00 CDN, $7.95 U.S.*

- **Wings of Wisdom: Your Daily Guide To Benefit From
  Change, Profit From Failure, and Design Your Own
  Destiny!**

*Why not make your life what you deserve? It doesn't matter at
what stage you are in life now, you can overcome debilitating
obstacles that jeopardize YOUR personal happiness, success
and the destiny you deserve. Discover the two things that can
dramatically change your life, the easiest way to change the
world, how to overcome fear, learn to profit from failure, how
to defeat procrastination, and a lot more! This book is your
template to guide you along the way.*
*ISBN 0-9683013-0-4. Hardcover, 266 pg. Includes references and
index. $23.95 CDN, $16.95 U.S.*

Volume Discounts Available Upon Request

Please add $3.00 shipping & handling for the first
book, plus $2.00 for each additional book

**Make cheque/money order payable to:
Anncath-Roby Books**
(Sorry, no C.O.D. orders)

Mail to:

**Anncath-Roby Books, P.O. Box 21085
Mississauga ON Canada L5N 6A2**

Order Form

Title	Cost Per Item	Quantity	Total
Wings for Goals	$11.00 CDN $7.95 US		
Wings for Work	$11.00 CDN $7.95 US		
Wings of Wisdom	$23.95 CDN $16.95 US		

Sub total _____

Add $3.00 Shipping & Handling for first book,
plus $2.00 for each additional book. _____

Cdn residents (excluding NB, NS, NF) add 7% GST _____

NB, NS, NF residents add 15% HST _____
(GST #87798 6455)

TOTAL ENCLOSED _____

Name: (Please print) _____

Address: _____

City: _____ Prov/State: _____ Country: _____

Postal/Zip: _____ Telephone: _____ (For order verification)

Register your e-mail address for new product information:

_____

Make check/money order (sorry, no COD orders) **payable to:**
Anncath-Roby Books
Mail to:

Anncath-Roby Books
P.O. Box 21085
Mississauga ON Canada L5N 6A2

**Guarantee: I understand that I may return any book for a full refund
for any reason up to 90 days after purchase, no questions asked.**